RV in UK

by
David Berry

By the same author:

'*The Motorcaravan Handbook*'

'*Tales from the Crewroom*'

'*The Whispering Giant in Uniform*'

Contents

Photographs are by the author

Introduction

This is a **personal** book; it is **my** view of American motorhoming in the UK. When I first thought of purchasing an RV, I wished I'd had a knowledgeable friend with whom to talk. There were the dealers, of course - and you will find that I am very supportive of them in this book - but that is not the same as sitting down for many hours and going into all the 'ins and outs' with an acquaintance.

I hope that you will regard the book in this light - I will tell you what I have learnt in these five years that I have been an owner and also pass on information that I have gleaned as a result of hiring RVs in North America. You will find that it is profusely illustrated and, because it is this personal guide, those photographs, and the text, are based on my own vehicles.

Whilst, when writing, I imagined myself talking to a novice, I think that many a seasoned RVer will pick up some tips and will also enjoy reading of the experiences of a fellow American motorhomer.

It will rapidly become clear that I am very pro-dealer. My view - and here we start that personal approach - is that it is essential to set up a good working relationship with a UK dealer. I have been extremely happy with the two I have dealt with. I have hesitated to name them as this would be unfair to those dealers of which I have no experience. I will leave you to make your own asssessment; there is a comprehensive list of the UK dealers in an appendix. Check them out and remember, whilst you are still a potential buyer, you have the advantage and then is

the time to determine what is on offer in the way of future care and support. This is an essential part of the operation of a large, expensive and complex vehicle. With a pre-read of this book you will be able to assess the after-sales service that you will require.

I hope too that the information given will help you choose the right RV for you. When you 'go for it', it is my view that you will be ahead of your time. I do believe that American motorhomes are going to become increasingly popular 'over here'. This will be driven by the increasing demand from British motorcaravanners for bigger vehicles of sophistication and quality. There is a move by European manufacturers to meet this market but, as the price of these approaches RV ones, then comparisons will be made and many people will choose to 'go American'. Doing this, you will be taking advantage of the years of experience of the USA manufacturers and the highly competitive North American market which means only the best survive.

The first couple of chapters will take you through all this. There then follows a step by step analysis of an RV's utility systems: gas, electricity and water - and appliances etc. There are a number of differences here between American and European motorhomes and these chapters will take the mystique away and show that there is really no great problem caused by these alternative ways.

The essential areas of engineering and driving are covered, followed by information on legal matters. There have been a number of changes made of late in this law area which have received a lot of alarmist attention. It is hoped that my interpretation of the regulations will help you see how the new legislation is of little consequence to the majority of UK American motorhome owners.

With all the foregoing dealt with, it will be time to think about getting on the road. Fitting out your RV is the first step and then deciding where to go. As this book is aimed at UK use, then the concentration is on suitable types of sites in this country. This should not detract from the book's value to those many RVers who take off for the Continental sun. After all, you still have to understand basic concepts - and your initial operation is going to be in this country.

However, Continental travel, and some of its implications, is touched upon.

I have said that I think the number of UK RVs will increase. I also believe that, with the growth, there will be another following of USA ways. Towing a car is extremely popular 'over there' and the advantages and simplicity will lead to it catching on here. A very full chapter is devoted to this topic.

The security of an expensive vehicle is a necessary subject. Having covered so many areas there are inevitably 'bits and pieces' left and that is the title of the penultimate chapter, the final one being on the USA scene - hiring and self importing.

Returning to my original statement: this **is** a personal book but through it I hope I convey a message. Using an RV in the UK is not that difficult and if you approach it with some of the obvious enthusiasm that I have, then you will thoroughly enjoy yourself.

Read on!

About the author
David Berry spent a lifetime as a pilot in the Royal Air Force. Towards the end of his service he developed an interest in writing and had published an anecdotal account of his flying days and a history of one of the transport aircraft he used to fly. With retirement, David and his wife, Valerie, took up motorcaravanning and have spent over a third of each year in their motorhome. They have travelled extensively in France, Spain, Germany and Austria as well as hiring in North America on four occasions. Back home, not a month goes by without a trip to some part of the country. He has used this experience to write for the motorcaravan press and in 1995 his 'The Motorcaravan Handbook' was published.

Think RV

Are you already a motorcaravanner and see an American motorhome and wonder what it's like to use one? Are you contemplating motorcaravanning and thinking of the possibility of going straight to a 'big one'? Are you just curious about all aspects of the great pastime of motorcaravanning? Whatever, what follows is for you.

The ethos

American motorhomes have 'something' that European motorcaravans do not. There is, of course, the size and the level of equipment. But there is more to it than that. One could say that it is all about them being American and that does lead to the nub of the matter. The market expectations in the USA are quite different to ours. This is not to decry our products; they have obviously developed to satisfy our expectations - but these are different in the USA. It is, perhaps, a measure of our conservatism that we do only have relatively modest vehicles. Does UK motorcaravanning still linger in the shadow of the Dormobile?

The price tag

It is no good starting to discuss American motorhomes without considering the vital factor of cost. They are more (much more?) expensive than their European cousins but there are a couple of things to take into account here. Firstly, like is not being compared with like. It will transpire in the pages that follow that the US specification is vastly greater. However, 'much more' was queried above because it is possible to spend as much, if not a little more, on a, top of the range, European motorhome but the American one will be far better equipped and have superior mechanical features. So, £ for £, you could be getting better value.

My father and his Dormobile circa 1955.

Please note that the term 'European motorcaravan' has been used throughout to describe the vehicles commonly available in the UK ie British, French, German etc.

The beginning of my downfall - the changeover from French Pilote to American Winnebago.

A 'by the way' - it is possible to spend an enormous amount of money on a totally 'over the top' RV but we are confining ourselves here to the more modest models - which are still lavishly equipped, by our standards.

A second point on cost is that one need not buy new. A study of the classified ads in the motorcaravan magazines will reveal a fair selection of secondhand models. It would seem from the details of some (age, mileage) that the sellers have bought new and found things not to their liking. One of the purposes of this book is to get prospective purchasers thinking about the implications of operating these larger vehicles. The people with 'bargains' for sale had obviously not given the matter sufficient thought beforehand. Perhaps they had not taken into account (particularly with partners in mind) that, for all its luxury, American motorhoming is still, essentially, just another form of the open-air life. This is not everyone's cup of tea. It is something for you to bear in mind. A partner's attitude is going to affect the amount of use. Another use factor is the amount of free time

that you have available. Some people might suggest that a large outlay would only be worthwhile if you were retired. You will be the best judge of your case.

So, to return to the original point, entry into the RV game is not solely via those expensive shiny new models - look around.

Self importing

Staying with cost, a thought crosses many people's minds (including mine), especially if they become aware of prices in the USA, 'Why not go to the States, buy one, use it there for a while and then bring it back to the UK?' This is discussed in Chapter 17.

Still going for it?

Spending so much money does require some thought but you can get enormous satisfaction and enjoyment from one of these vehicles - and after all, shrouds don't have pockets! I hope what follows will help with your choice of RV and answer all the questions that you have about operating one in the UK.

An example of a 'totally over the top' RV - but not an American one. This German model was alongside us at a campsite in Germany.

In boxes like this there will be asides.

Buying secondhand from a private individual perhaps requires some careful thought. An RV is a big commitment to take on without dealer backing?

The types

If you are familiar with the UK types of motorcaravans then this chapter will help (but might hinder) you in identifying the USA ones. To make things quite clear, and help those without motorcaravan knowledge, we will start from scratch.

The term luton originates from hat-making days in the town of Luton, Bedfordshire. Because of the completed hats' light weight, but relatively large bulk, a special design of van evolved which utilised the space over the cab. The shape became known as the 'Luton' - not many people know that!

Van types

There *are* American RVs based on commercial panel vans, although, from their luxurious appearance, it is difficult to identify those origins. Basically the manufacturer of the motorcaravan (the 'converter') has taken a panel van and fitted out the inside with furniture and appliances. If standing room inside is not available with the original vehicle then the manufacturer will probably have added a higher roof. In the UK these are known as 'high tops'. The American term is 'van camper' or a B-class (or Type B). When considering the USA types generally available in the UK, the van camper does not commonly feature.

Chopped vans

This term refers to the type where the converter has taken just the **cab**, engine and chassis of a commercial vehicle and built on the living element. The UK term is a 'coachbuilt' and they are a very common form of motorcaravan. They can usually be readily identified by an 'over the cab' portion which generally houses a double bed (albeit with limited headroom). We call this a *luton*. You will sometimes hear the American term of C-class used to describe this type of motorhome. Because they tend to be the smaller type of motorhome (although they can be as long as 28 feet), they are sometimes known, in the USA, as a 'mini-motorhome'. Finally, so that this guide is totally comprehensive, a last name for these is included - an 'over-cab' type.

With the American predilection for long distance travel, a chopped van, low profile type has

An American C-class or coachbuilt. It is the vehicle we hired for a fortnight in The Canadian Rockies. Hire in North America is discussed later.

been developed. It employs the same principle as the model above ie just the cab, engine and chassis being used but in this case a more streamlined living component is added. Inside, the impression is that driving convenience comes first with the living space having low headroom and being quite cramped.

The A-class

Left until the end is the type that most people would identify as American motorhomes. The A-class converter has just taken the engine, driving controls and chassis of the commercial vehicle (usually of quite a large van or lorry size or, not uncommonly, bus proportions) and on to this he has built a complete body, from front to rear. The styling of this is completely within his control so it might be seen that these vehicles can be more aesthetically pleasing than the C-class where a way has to be found of moulding the living component and the original commercial cab. There are internal considerations as well, which are discussed later.

These A-class types can be very large and luxurious. A length of 40 feet is possible but the more modest ones start at 24 feet. The larger ones can have a 'basement' ie the volume below the living quarters is dedicated to storage and houses all the systems ie tanks, heaters, generator and the like. These bigger RVs can also be 'pushers'; these have a rear-mounted engine.

Summary

Many names abound for the various types of RV but, essentially, the UK purchaser will be interested in two types: the C-class or coachbuilt and the A-class.

Which to choose?

Choosing between a C-class and an A-class falls into outside and inside aspects. If you want a smaller motorhome, say 24 feet to 27 feet, then you are likely to find more choice with the C-class. Conversely, if you are going for 'the big one' then it will be an A-class. The previously mentioned aesthetic aspect may decide you - beauty *is* in the eye of the beholder and I think A-class motorhomes win the looks' competition.

Inside the equipment levels will be very similar but the vital difference is in the layout. In an A-class the whole of the inside of the vehicle

A large A-class 'pusher' - a fellow resident at the old walled garden Caravan Club Site at Doune. These sites will be discussed.

converts to living space. A great feature of them is the driving seats. These 'captain's chairs' are extremely comfortable for the driving bit; when at rest they swivel and become wonderful armchairs. So, with an A-class, the driving area becomes very much part of the living area. This cannot be totally said of a C-class - a cab is a cab. However, the converters do go a long way to remove this feel when in the living mode. The driving seats might swivel.

Those A-class seats in the driving mode and turned into the living area.

The converse of this advantage/disadvantage can, perhaps, apply to the driving situation. With a C-class, you are in a relatively normal

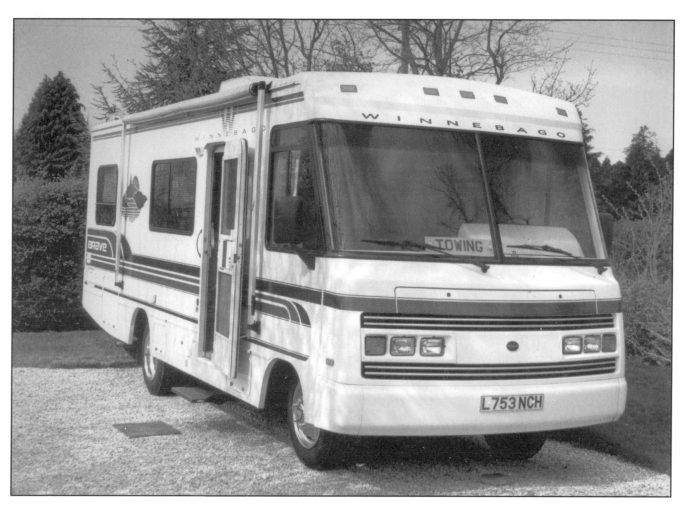

My first Winnebago
Brave 27RC - an
A-class - is going to
feature large in this
book ...

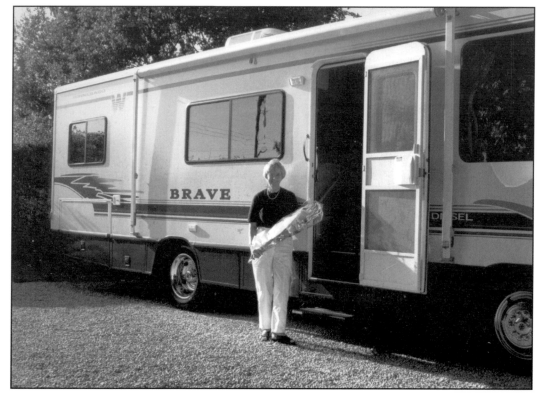

... but creeping in will
be its replacement, a
28RC. The bouquet
was a pleasant gesture
by the dealer.

driving environment - distance from windscreen and side windows, position of steering wheel, controls and instruments etc. This cannot be said of an A-class where you are in a driving position which takes some getting used to. With the construction of the whole body under the control of the converter then the driving compartment becomes a compromise between driving and living. You may have some reservation about this. It has been my experience that one does quickly get used to this different driving position - and, in fact, comes to relish it.

Power unit

The choice of engine, fairly obviously, is petrol or diesel. The argument for petrol is a cheaper-to-produce engine, one perhaps more flexible than a diesel, with a more rapid response. They are quieter. The down-side is that they are extremely 'thirsty'. These are big engines; eight or nine miles per gallon is pretty typical. In the USA, where gasoline is virtually a third of the UK price, this is not of such a consequence. I would suggest that here in the UK it does make the cost of journeys more than noticeable - you might consider 'prohibitively expensive' a more accurate description. So is diesel the answer? Well, it certainly offers a better mpg - you might get 15-16 miles from a gallon. (Unfortunately, the days of diesel fuel being cheaper than petrol are over in the UK but it can still be a factor in some Continental countries.) The drawbacks with diesel are that it is a more expensive engine to produce and might be considered more sluggish - although it does have the potential to produce more torque at lower revs. It is noisier than

petrol. Final warts and all - rectification of petrol might be more straightforward and cheaper but then, diesel has a reputation for long trouble-free life.

Which one?

It literally is a case of, 'you pays your money and you takes your choice.' Having said that, you will find that most of the UK dealers, who specialise in importing RVs, generally go for the diesel, probably, in the belief that most people would find the operating of a petrol too costly. But this did not seem the case in the past - possibly diesel-powered motorhomes were not so readily available. Anyway, for whatever reason, older secondhand RVs tend to be petrol-driven.

Other options

It has been indicated that the American motorhome comes lavishly equipped - 'fully loaded' is the term. In the USA, the system is much as ours - there is a basic model to which you add 'optional extras'. It does seem that the policy of UK dealers is to import models with all these optional extras fitted - 'Fully loaded, Sir!' This may be a little hard to take if you are trying to keep the cost down. The argument probably is that the extras, as a proportion of the total price, are not a lot and it is not worthwhile (or is difficult) obtaining and retro-fitting them. Whatever, when you have purchased, you will be more than pleased that you were forced to 'go the whole hog'! These accessories are analysed in a later chapter but next we will consider, in more detail, the difference between European and American motorhomes.

> A thought - for the lesser cost of a petrol engine against a diesel, how many gallons of petrol could you buy?

A photograph to muse on. Is a modest size RV so horrendously big? The estate is a Renault Savannah - the RV is 27 feet long.

The difference

The fundamental difference between the average American motorhome and a European motorcaravan has to be size. It is really around this that a different concept revolves. It also provides the biggest hurdle for the novice owner to clear.

Width thoughts! Whilst '100 inch' RVs have become 'the thing' in the USA, 8 feet vehicles are still being produced, perhaps with the export market in mind. '100 inch' is legal - just, but does this leave sufficient margin to add an awning? In the States, 102 inch RVs are now available; these **are** out-side UK and European limits. Finally, keep in mind, at 8 feet (and more so '100 inch'), you are as wide as a large goods vehicle.

Whilst we naturally associate things American with 'big', it is their market that has led to this development. They do, of course, have their much larger country in which to operate, but the size factor is the result of customer expectation. That demand, combined with a large market has created a very competitive trade and driven up quality and value for money.

That size

Contemplation of operating a large vehicle in our much smaller environment should be a concern. RVs can be very long - an average is 32 feet (9.8m). Strangely, height is not a really a problem; my Pilote, with a top box, was higher than the Winnebago, yet the headroom inside the latter (6ft 7in, 2m) is greater. But the most critical dimension for UK roads is width. The RV standard used to be 8 feet (2.4m); the maximum width for our 'normal use' vehicles was then 8ft 2in (2.5m). In the last couple of years, the Americans started producing '100 inch' wide RVs. This was going to create a difficulty here but EC regulations came to the rescue and

these wider motorhomes became legal on the back of an increase of permissible commercial vehicle width (2.55m, 100.4 inches).

Length has been brushed over. I do not think that this is critical on the road. My Winnebagos have only been 27/28 feet (8.2/8.5m) long but I would be quite happy now with a 32 footer. I specified 'on the road'; the extra length might prove a problem, now and then, site-wise.

The space

Is any inconvenience of this extra size of an American motorhome worth it? YES! Here comes a little bit of mathematics. Take a generous size UK coachbuilt with external length, width and height of 20ft x 7ft 2in x 9ft (6.1m x 2.2m x 2.7m). This gives, say, an internal floor space of 15ft x 6ft 8in (4.6m x 2.0m) and a headroom of 6ft 3in (1.9m) which equates to a cubic capacity of 625 cu ft (17.7m³). If the external width is increased to the RV's 8ft, giving 7ft 6in inside, then the capacity goes up to 703 cu ft - 78 more cubic feet, an increase of more than 12%. Now take a length of 27ft (American coachbuilt, say, so internally 22ft) and a headroom of 6ft 7in and the cubic capacity of the living space is 1086 cu ft - a massive 74% increase. The secret is that each extra inch of width or length or headroom also has the two other dimensions, so the effect is cubed. For comparison sake, it was assumed that the American was a coachbuilt. Think of the further increase in living area if it was an A-class. Confused by the numbers? Just step inside an RV and the immediate impression is of spaciousness.

Mechanical

To handle this greater size and weight requires some allowances in the mechanical department. It is here, particularly, that the American

'Only' eight feet wide!

manufacturers leave their European counterparts completely standing. In the UK the tendency is to use a commercial vehicle of the Peugeot Boxer, VW Transporter, Mercedes Sprinter, Renault Trafic type, with a 2.5 litre diesel as a typical engine. By the time the conversion has been carried out a considerable proportion of the basic vehicle's maximum weight has been used up with the weight of all the fixtures, equipment etc. Examine some of the payloads of these motorcaravans and you will find that they are quite small. If you pursue this subject you will find it very difficult to determine what has to be counted as payload by the owner - are water and gas included in the basic weight - or some of the accessories? All this adds up to operating very close to the limit, weight-wise - if not over it by the less than careful owner.

The Americans appear to begin at the other end of the scale. Instead of a commercial van they seem to start with something more in the lorry/bus class. A typical engine is a 6.2 litre diesel or 6.5 litre turbo-diesel. Owners are left in no doubt about weights. US law requires all the limiting weights to be placarded on the vehicle and the instruction manual will include a comprehensive breakdown of what is included in those weights. This provides the owner with full information on how much payload is available - not that this is really a cause of concern as it is so ample. This is the bonus of starting with a much more substantial base vehicle. It follows that the European motorcaravan is constantly operating at its upper limit, compared with an RV. This will be reflected in the wear and tear rates on the engine and other mechanical components. Motorcaravanners will vouch for the

Apart from the much larger engine sizes, there are other bonuses that are considered extras in the UK:

Power steering
Automatic transmission
Cruise control
Adjustable steering wheel

ease with which one can get stuck in a 'wet grass' situation - a situation caused by the predominance of front wheel drive in European motorcaravans. American motorhome are rear wheel drive - and double wheels at that.

I think the real give away in all this is the wheels - just look at those on 'one of our's' and compare them with 'one of their's'.

Money
So, we circle back to the matter of cost - this much higher mechanical specification should be very much taken into account when comparing prices.

Equipment levels
In the later chapters, much will be made of the equipment levels in American motorhomes; they will be considered in detail. In brief, it can be said that, as with the mechanical specifications, items that are listed as extras for European models are often included as USA standard.

Smoke detectors are a compulsory fit on our new motorcaravans; American motorhomes have a propane gas alarm and carbon monoxide detector as well.

A detailed weight sheet is included in Chapter10.

Smoke detector

Propane gas alarm

The plate that has to be affixed to the vehicle to conform with USA law. The gross vehicle weight maximum is shown as 14,500lbs (6,557kg). Weight is discussed in detail in a later chapter.

Examples of equipment etc, large and small, that come to mind are:

Generator.
Electric step.
Air conditioning (cab and domestic).
Hot water heating from the engine when on the move.
Rear heater when travelling.
Microwave oven.
Coffee maker.
Domestic clock.
Full size, separate shower.
Two domestic batteries.
Tow bar.
Remotely operated TV aerial with signal booster.
A 3 inch thick operations manual!
External TV point for connecting to a site aerial.
Bedside TV aerial socket + power supply.
Powerful extractor fan in the toilet roof vent.
Fly screens all round, **including door**.
Rear speakers for radio.
Rear ladder.
Spare wheel cover.
Fire extinguisher.
Venetian or pleated blinds at all windows.
Bed cover with matching cushion/pillows.
Settee loose cushions.

Some items are standard to both sides of the Atlantic but there are differences within those fittings:

A full-size permanently made-up double bed with a spring interior mattress.
A large capacity refrigerator with a separate large deep freeze.
Large oven with three/four burner hob.
Double stainless steel sink.
Much more storage space - particularly the wardrobe.
Big external lockers.
Almost an excess of roof and wall lights.

particularly strong on coordination - and that is everything - wall coverings, Formica tops, carpet, curtains, venetian blinds and upholstery.

Systems
There are a number of variations in the USA ways with gas, water and electrical systems compared with the European and in the next chapters these will be considered, in turn.

To the right: A full size separate shower plus marine type toilet. A DIY addition is wooden adjustable rods at the top of the shower cabinet for clothes/towel drying and airing.

A major difference is in the substance of construction components. The domestic door is taken as an example; the European ones have caravan origins reflected in their strength and the substance of the frame. The lock can be particularly poor. American motorhomes have a far more substantial door and **two** good locks.

I hope that the case for the greater superiority of the American motorhome has not been overstated! Is there any down-side? Well, it has to be said that not all American decor is to our taste. Some of it is quite garish with a preponderance of mirrors with curly designs and the like. 'You expect to find Gypsy Rose Lee sitting in some of them,' said one salesman. Winnebago are

In the USA, the term 'Recreational Vehicle' covers a number of different types. This is a 'Fifth Wheel' and is our USA resident son's outfit which we have borrowed. The coupling is on the floor of the load space of the truck. Its name is related to this type of coupling (the circular device is the 'fifth wheel') more familiarly associated with an articulated lorry. They are very popular in the States. The domestic fittings etc match that of a motorhome and there is the convenience of having transport when you are 'on site'. There are a few of these in the UK.

With thoughts turning to electricity, water and the dreaded sewage, it is as well to muse on the way things can be on a US campground and around which an American motorhome is designed. This is at Pipestem State Park, West Virginia. The box on the plinth is the electricity hook-up; the white pipe leads from the tap to the city water inlet on the RV (see later). The wide pipe goes into the pitch's own sewer outlet.

RV gas

There are some major differences between the American and European motorhome gas systems - but nothing that cannot be overcome.

Our way

If you are already a motorcaravanner then you will be familiar with our system of gas for cooking and heating being available in cylinders which are exchanged, empty for full. These are connected to the gas system with a flexible hose via a regulator. A variety of sizes are available and there are two types of gas - butane (in blue cylinders) and propane (in red). The latter is required for cold weather use as the liquid butane (gas cylinders contain butane or propane at pressures which turn the gas to a liquid) does not vaporise at low temperatures.

The system works well, particularly if you can carry two cylinders connected by a change-over valve for the time when the gas runs out in the middle of a rainstorm! One drawback is that there is no really simple dependable way of determining how much gas is remaining in a cylinder. A big plus is that if you use a well known make (Calor Gas is the obvious one) then you are never very far away from a replacement cylinder - in the UK. The

Continent is another story. ('*The Motorcaravan Handbook*' - see next chapter - has more detail.)

'Their' way

The American motorhome gas system is geared, not unnaturally, to the USA RV scene. The key there is bulk gas supply and, in the States, garages, campgrounds, RV dealers, fuel suppliers etc with this facility are 'ten a penny' (or should it be '10 for a cent'?). This is to match the fact that an American motorhome has a permanently fitted gas tank which has to be replenished directly from a bulk supply tank. There is a threaded inlet on the RV tank. The hose from the bulk tank, fitted with an on/off lever, is screwed into this and the liquid flows when the lever is squeezed. Several precautions have to be taken which are discussed later.

The tank

The capacity of the tank is large - typically 48lbs of liquid propane. My calculations (and eye ball) tell me that my Winnebago tank equates to two 13kg Calor Gas propane cylinders.

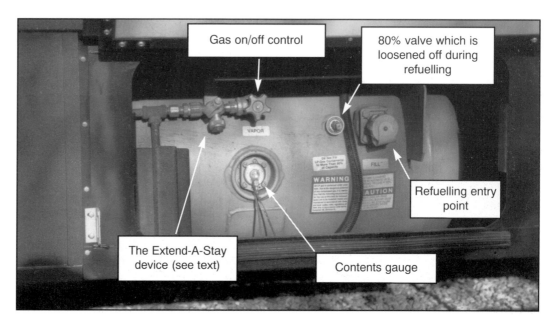

Gas on/off control

80% valve which is loosened off during refuelling

Refuelling entry point

The Extend-A-Stay device (see text)

Contents gauge

Behind a hatch cover is the gas tank with its controls.

(The **larger** of the European motorcaravans can accommodate two of this size cylinder.) My assessment of the RV's tank capacity is borne out by experience. A full one, in the summer months, can last six weeks - reducing to three or four in the winter. Talking of winter, note that you fill your RV tank with propane - the 'all temperature' gas.

A snag?

Can it be that some adverse comment is going to be made about American motorhomes? In use the gas system is totally convenient and has that long endurance - but when it is time for a refill, a the difficulty can arise. In the UK, retail outlets of bulk gas are a bit thin on the ground. So, a little planning is required. There **are** places with a bulk tank and it is a matter of keeping an eye on one's content gauge and arranging to be able to call on the supplier when the need arises. The most satisfactory way of finding the locations of suppliers is to ring your local Calor Gas regional centre. Lists of sources are published by magazines and owners' clubs from time to time but I have found these unreliable. The most likely suppliers are RV dealers; there are also some garages with tanks.

Having pointed out this drawback, something has to be said in defence. Firstly, you do not need replenishment that often and secondly,

Imperial measure is used in this book by default because you will find that this is the standard for figures in an American motorhome - lbs, gallons, feet and inches - the Americans are not having any truck with metric! One trap is that a US gallon is less than an Imperial one - 60 US gallons equates to 50 Imperial - this affects fluid ounces - their gallon contains 16 compared with our gallon containing 20. Add to all this the fact that, for comparisons in our market place, you have to convert Imperial to metric and it is difficult. Looking at the American motorhome gas tank, quantity-wise, and comparing it with our system, is a typical example of this problem. A conversion table is an appendix.

once you have found a convenient supplier, how many more do you need? The big thing is not to be caught out. You will find that you keep a wary eye on your contents gauge and I never let an opportunity to top-up (even though it might only be, say, less than half a tankful) pass by.

Help is at hand

There is, on the market, a device to assist you with this gas problem. It goes by the name of 'Extend-A-Stay' (a good Americanism) and it is designed to do what the name implies. It should be fitted by an expert who will tap into the pipe exiting the fitted tank a device which has a threaded fitting. Into this can be screwed a

When using Extend-A-Stay, to make things a little tidier, it might be possible to put the gas cylinder under the motorhome. This should be in the upright position. It is dangerous to use an LPG portable gas cylinder on its side.

This is the gas compartment of Winnebago No.1. A 13kg Calor Gas cylinder is connected to the RV gas system with the 'Extend-A-Stay' device. After connection, the hatch can be closed.

The multipurpose panel combines indicators and controls. The five columns of four black rectangles illuminate as red, amber or green lights. The two left columns are for the grey and black waste water tanks - green when E for empty - red when F for full. The fresh water, LP gas and battery condition columns have the lights in the opposite sense. The switches, left to right are for the water pump (PUMP ON light illuminates), the water heater (WH PILOT light illuminates if the flame does not ignite) and levels test. When this spring loaded switch is held on, the level indicators are active.

flexible pipe, the other end of which is attached to one of our standard propane gas cylinders - typically a Calor Gas 13kg one. The fitted tank main valve is turned to fully closed. A spanner is used to remove the sealing cap on the 'Extend-A-Stay' and the fitting on the end of the pipe is screwed into the vacant hole. This is tightened with a spanner. The other end is threaded (left-hand thread) on to the portable cylinder head and tightened. NOTE! You do **not** need a regulator; you are still using the one in the RV's system. With the main tank valve remaining closed, the one on the portable cylinder is opened. A wise precaution is to test your connections with a little soapy water. You are now in business, using gas from the Calor Gas

One Extend-A-Stay tip I can pass on is that I found it incredibly difficult to start the thread on the flexible pipe into the hole. I discovered that storing the pipe straight, as opposed to the natural way of coiling it, helped. I did this by keeping it in a cardboard tube. The tendency of the pipe will now be to remain straight whilst trying to start the thread. A further help is to keep it in the tube whilst you are turning the pipe.

(or whatever) cylinder. This is a tremendous system, allowing you to adopt a 'Scrooge' attitude towards your main tank contents!

Notice that another American motorhome plus has crept in - a gas contents gauge. You will find, in fact, that there are two. There will be a control panel in the motorhome with a gas indication. This will not be as accurate as the second one, which is on the tank itself.

Filling precautions

You will notice, in your motorhome and its manual, a proliferation of notices warning of death or serious injury if you do this or that - or, indeed, don't do this or that. It is a reflection of the 'suing for damages' state of US affairs. The gas tank is no exception. Perhaps mocking in this case is inappropriate as there are obvious dangers. Having said that, if there are incidents then they obviously don't happen on 'low news days'! Clearly, accidental ignition is a danger so the refuelling location should not be approached until the gas tank valve has been shut off and all appliances turned off. The only relevant ones I can think of are the refrigerator and pilot lights on the oven. Remember that there is residual gas in the pipelines. This would keep a pilot light going for quite a while. With the regard to the fridge, to my mind it is not a good idea for it to be trying to relight during the gas replenishment process, so put its control switch to 'off'. You may think of other safety precautions.

Things expand when they get hotter - the liquified gas in the cylinder is no exception. For this reason, the cylinder should only be filled to 80% of its capacity. This might seem difficult to judge but you will find that there is a screw on the tank which must be loosened during refuelling. When white vapour emerges from this then the tank is 80% full and the gas flow must be cut-off. The importance of this was reinforced for me when I was at a dealer's having my motorhome serviced. A fellow customer that day was having extensive work done to his gas system because it had been over-filled.

Refuelling is not usually a 'self serve' system so, call me 'over cautious' - I am always hovering, making sure that everything is in order. My beady eye is on that contents gauge. Mind you, the only problem I have ever had is persuading an 'attendant' to keep pumping. (The major difficulty here was that I am English and he was

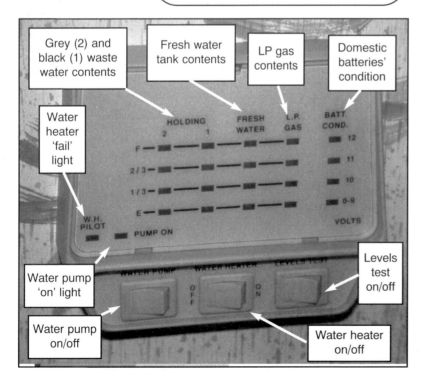

Grey (2) and black (1) waste water contents

Fresh water tank contents

LP gas contents

Domestic batteries' condition

Water heater 'fail' light

Water pump 'on' light

Water pump on/off

Water heater on/off

Levels test on/off

Austrian and there was not a lot in common on the language front!) He wanted to stop because he thought the tank was full because gas was coming from the 80% valve. This is normal - **gas** will be escaping but **liquid** is going in, so the proportion being lost is extremely small. The key is seeing vapour which indicates that the liquid level is reaching the 80% point.

You will find the American motorhome gas system is a safe and convenient one, once you have come to terms with the differences to our methods. There are some similar allowances to be made in the electricity department.

There is a gas/electricity connection in most UK RVs ie RVs that are diesel powered. In these vehicles the generator is run from the gas.

If you have an Internet access then, for sure, you will be exploring it to expand your RV interest. There is no doubt that, State-side, RVing is well represented. I have found nothing of immediate RV interest in this country apart from an Autogas site which lists locations of their bulk gas supplies! http://www.autogas.co.uk

Here are a few random US sites which might provide some links:

http:/www.tl.com	The site of the magazine 'Trailer Life', a premier US RV magazine.
http:/www.thetford.com	The Thetford toilet company.
http:/www.ndtourism.com	North Dakota tourism, which prompts the thought that the Net could be a useful source of information if you are planning a USA tour.
http:/www.campingworld.com	Camping World is a major USA RV accessories supplier.
http:/www.rvsearch.com	Secondhand RV market.

If you belong to CompuServe try **Go rvforum**.

RV electricity

As with gas, there are a number of differences with the electrical set-up in an RV and these are discussed in this chapter.

A continuing theme in this book is that two levels of knowledge are being dealt with: readers with no motorcaravanning experience at all and those with a European model background. For the former I would recommend my 'The Motorcaravan Handbook'. Even though it is based on 'our' motorcaravans, it will give some basic knowledge of systems etc (and general advice applicable to all motorcaravanning) that will provide a useful foundation for understanding an RV set-up. This chapter on electricity is an example of this.

The basics in brief

Electricity is an essential feature of modern motorcaravanning. It comes in two 'flavours' in a UK motorcaravan - three in an RV that has been modified for British use (see later). All motorcaravans have a 12 volt system, the power source being a 'domestic' battery ie a second battery in addition to the vehicle one, dedicated to providing that 12 volts for the living area. This means that in the event of there being no external power source (or that one is not being used as a matter of choice) then power is available for lighting, the water pump - and the limited use of 12v devices and a suitable TV; limited because a battery can only provide power for a certain length of time. The more power drawn off, the shorter that time. The battery is recharged, when on the move, by the vehicle alternator. This battery set-up is adequate for the simple use of a motorcaravan in the summer months which is all that some people require - or, indeed, seek after, as that sort of use would be associated with the smaller, quieter and more natural sites eg on farms.

If your requirements extend beyond this short-term use in favourable conditions then you will utilise the facility provided in all motorcaravans - a mains system. With this you plug into a site mains bollard or box (a hook-up) and then 240 volts is available at the power points in the motorcaravan and can be used for all normal domestic purposes (mains lighting and heating, TV, kettle etc and mains, instead of gas, running of the fridge) - providing you stay within the power limits of the supply (see later). The basic lights will still be on 12 volts but a charger for the domestic battery, running from the mains, will be replacing the used electricity.

The RV's third voltage

So, a European motorcaravan has a 12 volt and 240 volt system. A 'British' RV also has a 115/120 volt facility; this stems from its country of origin. In our houses 230/240 volts is the norm; in the USA it is 115/120. There are historical reasons for this difference. When an American motorhome is imported into this

The Motorcaravan Handbook

DAVID BERRY

'The Motorcaravan Handbook', a hardback with 160 pages, is published by Robert Hale and can be ordered from all good booksellers. ISBN 0 7090 5734 2

country it is mains wired up for 120 volts. The dealer has to carry out work to install 240 volts. This means the provision of a transformer, a ring mains with UK-type sockets and suitable protection devices. But some aspects of the 120 volt system have to be retained to run such things as the American fridge, microwave, coffee maker, battery charger and air conditioner (though on some models intended for the UK market, the latter can be 240 volts). The result of all this is the **three** voltages in a 'British' RV - 12, 120 and 240.

Batteries

Car knowledge will give you an idea of the endurance of a 12 volt battery - how long can you leave your headlights on before the battery is flat? If you are without mains hook-up, the challenge is to manage your electricity use within the capacity of the battery. This is eased somewhat in an RV in that there will be at least two domestic batteries of quite high capacity. Some of this advantage is eroded by the fact that, because of the sophistication of the equipment, the consumption can be higher. One thing to keep in mind is that two appliances that can be, or are, run from the gas, eg the fridge and the blown air heating, need a 12 volt supply for their electronic control. So, you may have a tankful of gas but your fridge won't run if your domestic batteries are flat.

The generator

But help is at hand; undoubtedly your RV will have a built-in generator with a good output (3+Kva is typical). If your motorhome is petrol-driven then the generator will also run from petrol. In the more likely event that you have a diesel engine then the generator will run off the gas. We have already seen that in the UK your gas tank contents are something of a precious commodity so be advised that the gas consumption rate of the generator is quite high. But it is there for that time that you are heading for a flat battery problem. Your generator can have a 120 or 240 volt output - some manufactures fit ones with the latter to export models. In this case, the plug that you normally connect to the mains hook-up is plugged into the generator; the connection will be in the cable compartment. Then, through your mains system, it will run all your appliances as if you were plugged into normal mains - but you have to stay within the output capacity of the generator. Follow the instructions in the generator's literature. One point that

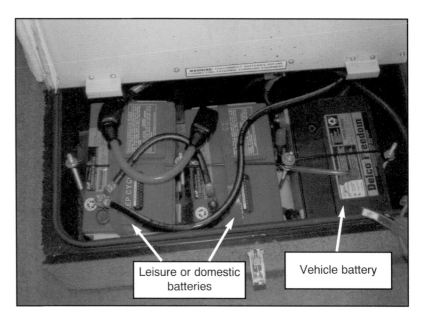

Leisure or domestic batteries

Vehicle battery

will be made is that you should start the generator with no electrical loads demanded and let it warm-up before applying them. The reverse should be the case for the shut-down ie switch off all the appliances etc and let the generator run for a while before shutting it down.

Looking down on the underfloor battery compartment of an RV. The Delcro Freedom battery to the right is the vehicle one. The two on the left are the deep cycle leisure or domestic batteries.

A hook-up bollard at a Caravan Club Site. The top portion is a light illuminated at night. I hasten to point out that it is not my cable evidently under some strain! I have a loop taped into mine which greatly assists tidy and caring coiling. When disconnected, I walk forward with the cable, going hand over hand using the pre-taped loop as a guide. The reverse process is used when connecting up. This eliminates tangling and kinking the cable.

The generator in its Winnebago No.1 exterior locker. With this installation it can be started in three places: on the driver's console, with a switch on the oven hood and at the set itself.

The short cable, connected to the motorhome mains system, is hanging out of the cable compartment and is connected to the cable going to the site hook-up. When everything is set up then, for weather protection and tidiness, the socket and plug connection can be put in the compartment and the door closed.

My own driveway hook-up using the short cable.

Keep in mind that generators are not the most popular devices with some of your fellow nomads. The persistent noise can be something of an irritant in quiet rural situations. Admittedly an RV's generator is something of a more subdued affair than the free-standing ones on the market - but don't push that point. Use it during 'sensible' hours to just charge up your batteries - we find, in a 'field' situation, an hour at late breakfast-time is acceptable - and it lets you use the toaster as well. Running it for hours in the evening so that you can watch TV is likely to 'get up the nose' of the occupier of that little VW camper who is within earshot!

Mains hook-up

Part of the dealer's electrical modification will be a UK-style cable to connect to a site bollard. The standard US way of doing this is to have a cable (borrowing a term from boating, it is known as a 'shore line') permanently connected to the input point on the motorhome circuit - also the cable is not very long compared with ours (reflecting their typical pitch set-ups - we can sometimes be a long way away from the bollard and a 25 metre cable is our standard). My dealers followed the US pattern and permanently wired the cable into the system. I found it very inconvenient trying to store this longer cable in the housing provided. I have also found it handy to be able to use different length cables. So I cut the cable at about the 2 metre point and installed a plug. This very short cable is easy to coil into the compartment and plug into the generator. In my driveway I have installed my own mains outlet and it is located so that this short cable reaches it. On a site, depending on the distance from the hook-up bollard, I can decide whether I need my standard 25m cable, or one of medium or short length.

Loads

The capacity of a mains hook-up, at its best, can be 16 amps but it might be only six (even four on the Continent). With a European motorhome it is quite easy to exceed this - with an American one it is even easier! Get to understand what the draw of your appliances are - generally speaking, using electricity for heating means more amps. If you use a fan heater, electric kettle and toaster all at once then you are more than likely to trip the supply. The number of amps being drawn can be calculated by dividing the wattage of the device by the volts eg a 1kw (1000 watts) heater on 240 volts draws 4.2 amps. A fuller

The story goes that when the electricity companies were being set up in the USA they were in competition with the existing gas firms. The latter put it about how dangerous electricity was which forced the electricity producers to lower the voltage to persuade the public on safety. Mind you, 120 should still be treated with respect. From where do the figures 230/240 and 115/120 come? In each respective country the power station produces 400 and 200 volt **three** phase. Domestic situations only use one of those phases. The voltage of a single phase is the original three phase voltage divided by the square root of the number of phases ie 400 or 200 divided by the square root of 3 - QED!

explanation of all this is given in '*The Motorcaravan Handbook*'.

Frequency

To keep technicalities to a minimum, please accept that an electricity supply, as well as having the aforementioned voltage specified, also has a frequency. This, like the voltage, differs between ourselves and the USA. Our 240 volts has a frequency of 50Mhz; the USA 120 is 60Mhz. This is only of concern in two areas. A poor (cheaper?) 240 volt dealer conversion that does not take account of this can be noisy; it is the transformer. I have read of some UK RV owners who have to turn the mains off at night because of this! So, check the intentions of your dealer. The second (minor) snag is that US electric mains clocks do not run at the correct speed on our supply. Our microwave in the first Brave had such a clock. For sanity's sake we did not set it and then 1200 was permanently displayed.

Battery maintenance and precautions

Keep an eye on the fluid levels in your batteries. I think that I fuss over my Winnebago but, to my eternal shame, one summer I let the battery levels get very low. The rate of drop can be quite high. Mine is accelerated by the fact that I keep the mains permanently plugged in when at home. Some owners don't like doing this but I find it necessary for an auxiliary alarm system (see later) and I also like to run a small heater in the winter. It also ensures that the domestic batteries are permanently charged up.

On a hook-up, the vehicle battery is **not** charged. It does seem that with an RV, even though everything, vehicle-wise, is 'turned off', there is still some drain on this battery - in my flying days we called them 'standing loads'. If the RV is left unused for three to four weeks then these loads could totally drain the vehicle battery. Periodic charging is called for. The

totally correct way of doing this is to remove the battery from the vehicle and connect it to a battery charger. You can decide for yourself whether this is being ultra-cautious and take instead one of two alternative routes. If you connect the positive terminal of your domestic battery to the positive terminal of the vehicle one with a cable having crocodile clips at each end then the vehicle battery will be replenished by the RV's battery charger. You will read that you should disconnect the vehicle battery before charging but I have been advised that the rate at which the RV system charges is not likely to cause any harm to the engine's electronic components. One point that needs care is to remember to remove the cable before turning the engine - the high starter motor loads will melt the cable and cause a fire hazard. It would pay to wire a fuse into the cable to guard against this and other malfunctions.

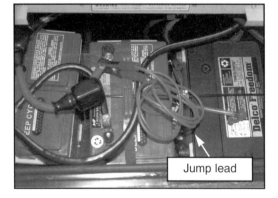

Jump lead

A jump lead joins the positive terminal of the 'end in the chain' domestic battery to that of the vehicle one.

An alternative to this 'jump lead' method is to have a dedicated normal charger. The one I purchased in Halfords fits in the battery compartment and lives there permanently. When charging time comes, I simply connect the leads to the terminals and the mains plug to a nearby RV mains socket. Whether you adopt either of these somewhat maverick methods is your decision!

Hook-ups come in many forms; the one on the right needed some protection from sheep, it being on a CL. CL? They will be discussed later.

An RCD

A 120 volt double socket incorporating a GFCI.

Circuit breakers and fuses

You will be able to identify a component of the RV's original electrical system; this is a power converter (photo p34), a transformer and rectifier. It will also contain 120 volt circuit breakers. The transformer drops incoming 120 volt down to 12 and rectifies it from AC to DC. This 12 volts is then used for the 12 volt systems eg lights, water pump, and to run the charger for the domestic batteries. Get to know this box. I found it useful to switch off each circuit breaker, one at a time, and identify their function. The box also contains fuses for the 12 volt system; these too should be identified. Having done this, then make a list and stick it to the door of the compartment, for future reference. You might sometimes be aware of a noise coming from this box. This will be the battery charger, and its cooling fan, running. Other fuses to get to know are those associated with the base vehicle eg sidelights, windscreen wipers etc. You may also find some 'domestic' fuses here. In my Winnebago the fuse for the propane gas leak detector was amongst them and it is useful to be able to use this to isolate the device, for long term storage, to eliminate drain on the battery.

Leave yourself a note to remember to replace the fuse before using the RV again.

RCD

Close by the American electrics box, the UK dealer will have placed a 240 volt protection device(s) - a residual current device (RCD). This will probably look familiar to you, being borrowed from the house electrics scene. The purpose of an RCD is to instantly detect an electrical fault and, equally instantly, cut off the supply. This makes them somewhat sensitive devices.

Ground Fault Circuit Interrupter

A GFCI is an American protection device and you will find at least one in your 120 volt system. They take the strange form of being part of a normal socket (the Americans call these receptacles). One or more of your sockets will have a red button. If the protection system is activated then the button pops out and that circuit (not just that socket) is dead. If this happens, I would be inclined to unplug all the appliances on that circuit, reset the GFCI by pushing the button back in and then reconnecting the appliances one at a time to see if you can identify which one is at fault. Beyond doing this, I would seek expert help.

Bulbs

Personal experience again comes to the fore with the subject of lighting. The bulbs in the numerous RV light fittings are 12 volt so even when you are on mains hook-up, they still run off a 12 volt supply. However, in my Winnebago it is noticeable that these lights are much brighter when on hook-up than when running from the domestic battery; this indicates that they are slightly over-volted in the hook-up case. This is borne out by the seemingly short life of some of the bulbs. I have installed supplementary mains lights - this need not be complicated: a table lamp, clip-on spotlights - or if you feel more ambitious (and have the knowledge) more permanent style lighting can be installed. I have wired up permanent mains lights above the washbasin mirror, over the settee and on a wall. Apart from the superior lighting from normal bulbs, it saves on the 12 volt ones!

When you are seeking replacement 12v bulbs, then buy with caution; they **are** automobile bulbs but particular ones. Examine the original and you will see that the securing pins are at the same level and there is only one filament. Many automobile bulbs have a double filament and the pins are staggered so that the bulb can only be inserted one way in its holder. You do not want

either of these types. Check the contacts on your bulbs; they either have a double contact on the base or a single one. My Winnebago fooled me here; the roof lights are a single contact and the wall lights double. It is easy to choose what looks like the right bulb from motor accessory stock but it can have the wrong number of contacts, pins at different levels and more than one filament! Halfords always has a good range and the code number that suits my Winnebago is Type 335 for the wall lights and Type 382 for the roof ones. These are 21 watt bulbs. If you want a gentler light then 10 watt ones are available (Type 245). Some of the roof type lights have two bulbs on the same switch - which is two-position. The first switches on one light and the second, both. It can be useful to put a low wattage bulb in position one, for subtle lighting, and a higher one in the second.

An essential part of your travelling kit should be spare bulbs - both for the vehicle and the domestic area - and spare fuses.

Finally

Electricity is a wonderful facility in any motor-caravan but never more so than in an RV. With the great range of installed and added equipment one can live conveniently in real comfort.

Having considered gas and electricity, the only remaining utility is water - which is the next topic.

A mains downlight located on the underside of a locker to shine down on the settee.

Compare this photograph with the one on page 23. The two leisure batteries, on the left, have been re-arranged and a larger vehicle battery, on the right, fitted. It is my belief that American batteries are not as good as UK ones. This was borne out for me when my Winnebago one failed after three years; in its life before that it was not that hot, going flat in what seemed a short time. The advice I received about a replacement was, 'Fit the biggest one that will go into the compartment!' So, the leisure batteries were moved and this left room for a 90 amp/hr Lucas commercial vehicle battery. It has been very satisfactory.

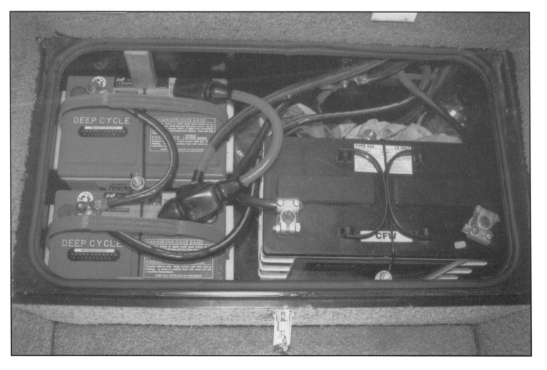

RV water

There have been some major differences pointed out with the gas and electrical systems installed in an American motorhome. Similar variations continue into the water arena.

Tanks

Almost all European motorcaravans have two water tanks - one to store fresh water for the taps at the sink and the washbasin and for the shower head - and one for the waste water from those locations. The water pressure at the taps is provided by a 12 volt pump which switches on automatically when a pressure drop in the system is sensed due to a tap being turned on. There will be an exterior filler for the fresh water tank and a discharge point for the waste water one.

In all this, the RV is similar - but bigger! And there is an additional waste tank. A typical capacity of an RV's fresh water tank is 54 US gallons = 45 Imperial gallons = 205 litres. A large UK motorhome has a 100 litre tank. The two waste water tanks are for grey water and black water. Grey water is the discharge from the sinks, washbasin and shower - capacity 40 US, 33 Imperial, 151 litres. The black water is from the toilet - 35 US, 29 Imperial, 132 litres. This latter tank is a major difference between UK and US and replaces our cassette toilet system where the sealed 'cassette' can be removed and taken to a discharge point for emptying. With the US system the whole RV has to be driven to the emptying point. This might seem a major drawback but look back at those capacities again. We find that for the two of us the contents of all the tanks comfortably cover our needs for, at the very minimum, six days and can be spun out to even longer with judicious

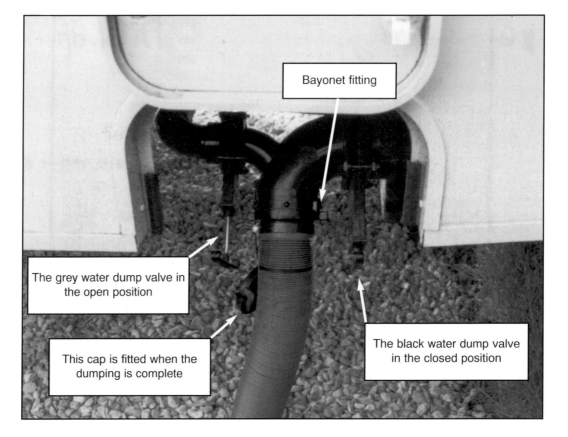

A close-up of the dumping valves. Coming in from the top left is the 2 inch pipe from the grey water tank. Its dump valve is open. To the right the 3 inch pipe for the black water. with the valve closed Centre is the flexible pipe connected by a black plastic bayonet fitting. Hanging behind it, partly concealed, is the cap for the discharge point.

Bayonet fitting

The grey water dump valve in the open position

This cap is fitted when the dumping is complete

The black water dump valve in the closed position

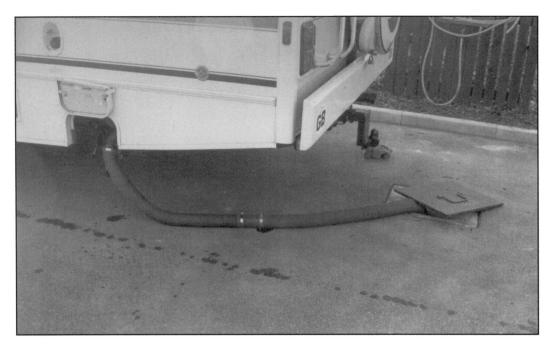

Dumping at a Caravan Club Site 'MV Waste Point'. There are two points to note. Firstly, the extra long hose made up of two pieces joined together. Because of vehicle size and the location of its dumping valves and where the ground drains can be positioned, this length is often necessary, as in this case. The second point is that the drain cover is being used as an anchor. The force with which the contents of the tanks are discharged is quite alarming and the end of the pipe could easily be whipped out of the hole unless some precaution is taken.

use. Although this 'dumping' might seem a snag, one only has to experience the cleanliness and convenience of the discharging system to be completely won over and be prepared to accommodate any time limit or RV moving to dump.

Dumping

The outlets from the grey and black water tank come together at a 3 inch diameter discharge hole. This has two lugs on it to which can be connected the bayonet fitting on the end of a flexible pipe. This comes in various standard lengths. It is useful to have one about 3 feet long and one extra long one (12+ feet formed by joining two shorter lengths). At the disposal point (the 'dumping station' in US terminology) the pipe is secured to the RV's discharge point and the other end put into the drain. There are two valves, one for each of the waste tanks. The larger (3 inch) one is for the black water and this is opened first. In a matter of literally seconds the contents will have been discharged. That valve in then closed and the adjacent smaller (2 inch) grey water one opened. Apart from emptying the grey water tank, this water is flushing out any black water nasties in the pipe. With the grey tank empty, the pipe is removed and stowed and the sealing cap screwed back onto the RV's discharge point. All that is required now is the addition of the chemical toilet fluid to the black water tank. Given a convenient dumping station this can all be accomplished in minutes. The guy with his cassette toilet is still carrying his plastic box around the site!

Precautions

The simplicity of all this should not create an air of complacency. Even though one is isolated from it, always keep in mind that 'nasties' are being dealt with. Wear a pair of waterproof gloves that are kept specially for the purpose. Check before you open that black water valve that the tank contents are going to go where you intend. The discharge is quite forceful, which is a good thing, but it can easily throw the end of the pipe out of the drain hole. Put the pipe well down the hole and weight it down with something - perhaps the metal cover for the discharge point or a handy large stone. When I pull that handle, my hand stays ready to immediately close the valve should there be a problem. At a well organised site there will be an adjacent tap and hose for flushing whilst and after dumping - be generous.

Your black water tank requires some long term care. If you peruse American RV accessory catalogues you will see many devices for flushing out the inside of the tank. Perhaps just the end of a hose down the toilet will suffice (keep a short length dedicated to this purpose to join on to the end of your normal hose - remember, at all costs, you have to prevent contamination). I look for occasions when I can arrange to travel with the black water tank two thirds full of clean water and toilet fluid. On the journey it can have a good slosh around and then be dumped. At home I occasionally fill the tank with clean water, dump, refill, dump - a number of times.

The disposal points provided for cassette toilet emptying are usually too high off the ground for RV dumping. A solution to the problem is to fit a macerator pump which allows the contents of the black water tank to be pumped through a relatively narrow pipe.

My dumping station. An underground pipe was installed from the edge of the drive to an inspection pit. The inlet is a rodding eye which provides a suitable cover when the drain is not in use.

To the right is a wheeled toilet emptying tank. A short flexible pipe connects the waste outlet to the tank. When the tank is full the pipe is disconnected and a cap fitted. This tank should be used at intervals ie do not leave it connected with the dump valve open.

Make up your own tool, from a bent nail and piece of wood, for lifting drain covers

To the far right: A convenient carrying place for the tank is on the rear ladder.

A farmer's toilet emptying provision which is not suitable for RV dumping because of the height from the ground. But beside it is a drain cover which will suit the purpose very well.

I have constructed my own 'dumping station' - a spur to the nearest house drainage inspection chamber.

The grey water tank does not present the same germ problem but smell could be a difficulty. A good fill/dump/fill/dump routine does not hurt here either. The addition of some toilet fluid to this tank, now and again, can be beneficial.

This waste water system does take a little getting used to and requires some thought but after a while you will be swearing by it.

What if ...

There can a big 'what if' with the system. You can find very occasionally, when you are touring, that the RV is going along with the equivalent of its legs crossed! It is days and days since you have been able to dump and there never seems to be a suitable point. Happily, site operators, The Caravan Club in particular, are

Cassette toilet dumping

Drain cover

increasingly making provision for motorhomes with ground level discharge points - the ones for cassette toilet emptiers are no good for us as they are generally 2 to 3 feet off the ground. If that is all there is then look for an adjacent inspection pit cover. You may be able to lift this and dump there - I suggest you ask the camp owner or warden first!

A solution to the problem, and one that will also come to your rescue if you do not wish to move your RV for an extended period, is a wheeled waste tank - Fiamma make one. This has a short pipe that provides a sealed link between the RV

drain and the tank. When emptying time comes, the black tank valve is opened and as the tank contents rise, a little float indicator pops up to indicate that the valve should be closed. With the pipe removed from the tank and a cap put in its place, it is time to join the 'cassette men' for the trek to the emptying point. By the time you have done this a number of times you will be fully appreciating the convenience of your normal system - if you hadn't done so already.

Fresh water

The fresh water system of an RV is fairly straightforward. The tank is filled from an exterior point which has a lockable cover. It can take some time to load 200+ litres. You should use food grade hose to do this. Your RV supplier will have imported US ones which are white in colour. They have screw fittings each end, one to suit the USA standard campground tap; the other matches the fitting for RV city water (see

Smaller supplementary cap to take a hose fitting

Notice that this main sewer outlet cap has a subsidiary cap which, when unscrewed can accept a hose with a screw fitting. Appropriately, this is called a 'cheat valve' as it can be used for dumping grey water into a hedge etc. One needs to be very guarded about its proper use; in a field might be OK but on a site it would not be at all acceptable.

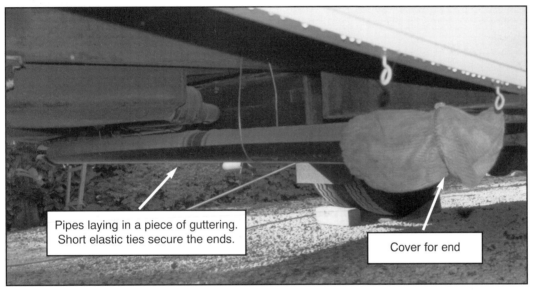

Pipes laying in a piece of guttering. Short elastic ties secure the ends.

Cover for end

Carrying dumping pipes can be a bit of a problem. Investigate the underside of your RV and you will find tons of room for some sort of stowage system. Here I used simple guttering. I did install something more sophisticated in my new Brave - a couple of pipes complete with end caps - see Chapter 16.

below). You might find it useful to cut these off, leaving about 6 inches of the pipe, and to fit our

> I use garden hose because that is what is fitted to a Hozelock, through flow, hose box which I find very convenient. It takes 20 metres of hose but you do not have to unreel it all. Just take the hose box to the tap and connect what is normally the delivery end to the tap. Now walk back to the RV, unwinding as you go. At the refill point put the shorter length of hose, which is the bit normally attached to the tap, in the hole - and start filling. No more struggling with a recalcitrant hose.

Hozelock couplings. With a selection of these you are ready to meet the challenge of the variety of taps that you will come across. One unfortunate feature of these USA hoses is that they are incredibly difficult to neatly coil up and they kink very easily. So, I have to confess that I use the more manageable garden hose but I fetch all my drinking water in a two litre container. This is not that tedious as it is surprising how little water one actually drinks!

The USA scene

We have considered gas, electricity and water - the USA campground scene has to be pictured to understand how these systems have developed. A campground of any size will have a bulk gas supply. Your pitch will have an electricity hook-up, a water tap and a sewer outlet - all for your exclusive use.

RV things improve with the years. The dump valves of No.2 Winnebago are contained in a locker, which guards against frost. All the water tanks are also inboard.

This raises a couple of points. Firstly, we have to return to the dreaded toilet waste scene. If you are ever are in the situation where you have your own sewer outlet then do not be tempted to have your discharge pipe permanently connected with the valve open. Leave the pipe connected, by all means, but keep the valve closed and dump at intervals, more or less as normal. Without having to go into too much sordid detail, I will leave you to appreciate that the contents of the tank needs emptying with some gusto - you don't want 'stuff' lying about!

Moving to a more pleasant topic, your own fresh water tap is pretty much standard in the States and is a considerable asset which will become increasingly available here. If you do have such exclusive use then you can take advantage of the RV's 'city water' facility. This strangely named system starts with a threaded female inlet somewhere low down on the outside of the RV. To this is attached the standard US hose by means of the pre-fitted threaded male end. Now with the other end attached to the permanently turned on tap (and the RV water pump turned off), mains water is available at all the taps - a wonderful noiseless system! There are two points of care and they both concern protecting your pipes and fittings against over-pressure and surge which could cause damage. Only turn the outside tap on sufficiently to provide adequate water flow at the RV tap. This will keep the water pressure down; a better way is to fit a pressure limiting valve which your RV dealer might stock. The second way to protect your system is to guard against a back surge when you disconnect. First turn off the outside tap, then open an RV tap until the water ceases to flow, ie no pressure in the line, then disconnect the pipe. City water has a useful function in connection with winter precautions; these are discussed later.

What else?
A chapter is now called for to look at the various appliances and miscellaneous fittings in and on your 'dream machine'.

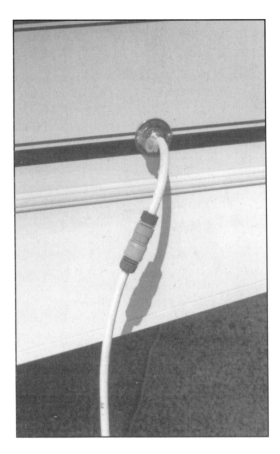

The photograph to the left shows the 'city water' connected. Note the Hozelock fittings for adapting the hose to various situations. To the right is the latest thing in bollards! Added to the normal electricity is a water connection and, on the side, a TV signal supply.

Below is a brand new 'mv waste point'. This and the bollard above were photographed at one of The Caravan Club's latest Club Sites at Edinburgh.

Appliances, fittings and accessories

It has been said that you will find that an RV is generously equipped. In this chapter some of these 'goodies' are examined.

The fridge.

In line with US homes, your RV fridge will be big - typically 4+ cubic feet. There is likely to be a separate deep freeze also of generous proportions. It has already been stated that the fridge can be run from the mains or from the propane gas. In a sample make (Norcold) there is a control switch marked 'Auto', 'Off' and 'Gas'. For normal operation the switch is left at 'Auto'; in this position the fridge will operate from the mains (if available) and a red 'AC' will be illuminated. If the mains should fail, then there will be an automatic changeover to gas operation and a red 'LP' displayed. If, for some reason, you wish to operate from the gas even though mains is available then the switch should be placed to 'Gas'.

I find this position useful when the gas has been

turned off for some time and I am preparing for a journey. Firstly, the fridge is run, on the mains, for 24 hours beforehand, to pre-cool it. Then, when the mains supply is removed for the journey, I want to be sure that the fridge switches to gas operation - but this might fail because there is air in the supply lines. (Failure to ignite is indicated by the illumination of a small red cross.) To ensure that the automatic changeover will take place, select the coldest temperature on the fridge control panel and switch to 'Gas'. Watch for the red cross illuminating. If it does, then put the control switch to 'Off', pause, and then reselect 'Gas'. Keep doing this until the red cross does not light up. This indicates that the gas flame in the cooler unit is lit - if you listen carefully you can hear the noise of the flame. Return the switch to 'Auto' and the temperature control to its normal setting. Now, when the

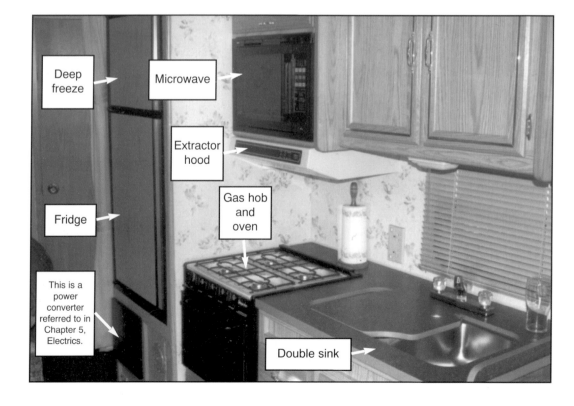

A well equipped RV kitchen with fridge, deep freeze, microwave, oven hood complete with extractor fan. The gas stove has four hobs. Bottom right is the double, stainless steel sink with worktop cover.

Deep freeze

Microwave

Extractor hood

Fridge

Gas hob and oven

This is a power converter referred to in Chapter 5, Electrics.

Double sink

mains is disconnected, there will be gas available at the cooler unit.

When you are using your RV, experiment with the fridge temperature control setting. Clearly, you want to run the fridge at what is the most reasonable lowest setting. It is very easy to have too cold a temperature selected; the contents of the fridge will freeze.

Fridges of old had to be pretty level to function. Nowadays, if you are level enough for comfortable occupancy then this will be OK for the fridge. However, if you are parked in the road, or whatever, at an angle (fore and aft or side-to-side) and intend staying more than an hour then the fridge should be turned off to prevent malfunction and damage to the cooling unit.

Another personal experience! The first time we used our Winnebago we experienced winds of 90 mph! As we sat in our rocking home there was horror as we saw water seeping onto the floor at the bottom of the fridge. What was happening was due to the fridge ventilation vents on the outside of the RV. These are obviously not designed to keep out horizontal Welsh rain and the back of the fridge was soaking wet; water was seeping through gaps where it had been installed in its housing. I later sealed these with a waterproof flexible filler. This was not the end of our difficulties with these vents. Some months later we were side-on to high winds and Welsh rain again. Once more, the compartment was saturated and this shorted out the electrics. I fitted an angled rigid plastic shield to take the impact of the rain. This might have interfered with the ventilation but, 'touch wood', it seems to be OK and the fridge essentials are now kept dry.

During storage, look after your fridge. Always be meticulous with cleaning - food smears etc will create a mildew problem. Leave the door of the fridge and deep freeze slightly open. On the control panel there might be a switch marked 'Normal Operation', 'Storage ' and 'High Humidity'. Put the switch to 'Storage' to ensure that all power supplies to the fridge are isolated. (The 'High Humidity' position should be used if there is evidence, during normal use, of condensation around the door surround.)

You will enjoy the tremendous convenience of a large refrigerator and deep freeze.

Cooking

Generosity of size in the 'keeping cool' area extends into 'heating up'. RV ovens, with their four gas rings, are big. My Winnebago rings are simplicity itself - turn the control knob to HI LITE and apply a light (a gas gas-lighter is a handy thing to have). Some hobs might be fitted with automatic ignition. Turning the control back towards the off position will lower the flame.

The oven control knob has, in clockwise order, a pilot light position, then temperature marks (in Fahrenheit) and, finally, a BR position, which is for broiling (more later). It is possible, but a bit of a fiddle, to light the pilot light with a match,

The two horizontal vents for the fridge.

or whatever, with the control knob in the 'pilot' position. The easiest thing to do is turn the control to a temperature and ignite the whole oven main burner ring. When use of the oven is complete, and you wish to keep the pilot alight for future use, then only turn the knob back to the pilot position. When the oven is required again, simply turn the control to the required temperature and it will ignite. The main flame will cycle on and off to control the temperature. When travelling, the pilot light should be turned off.

Broiling is the US term for grilling but we have found that it does not produce the same results as the grills on our ovens. It is probably the absence of a glowing red grill. To 'broil', the control is turned to BR and the food is placed beneath the main burner ring. With the control at BR, the oven thermostat is by-passed and the

The mini-oven permanently installed with its heat protecting shield. We found it better, later, to keep it in a cupboard and use on the worktop when required.

To the right is the familiar bulge of an RV's air conditioner.

A ceiling vent of a modern RV air conditioning system.

It might strike you that the outside component of the conditioner seems rather exposed in the winter months. It is possible to buy tailored covers.

main burner ring is alight the whole time. It might be us but this does not seem to 'grill'. We have overcome the problem with a small electric oven. The 'broiling' problem led us into this but we would not be without one of these mini-ovens now. Firstly, it **does** grill; secondly, it makes toast (so out goes the toaster) and thirdly, it is so often convenient to just use the small oven and not have to light up the gas oven - and, finally, you are using the electricity that you have paid for rather than the gas! No motorcaravan should be without one.

If you are an experienced motorcaravanner then you will know that cooking moisture must be dispersed. Your RV will have a cooker hood with an oven light and an efficient extractor fan, albeit, possibly, a somewhat noisy one.

Air conditioner

Many of the comparisons that have been made between UK and US are along the lines of 'similar, but bigger and better'. With air conditioning it is a comparison with the non-existent! It has to be admitted that there are very few UK occasions which justify air conditioning - but you will have it for those rare events and it can be most welcome - and there is the Continent. There will be an air conditioner for the 'cab' area and one for the domestic. The former is for use when you are on the move and is simply an extension of the normal fresh air/heater controls. The domestic conditioner will run off the mains, either at 120 volt via the transformer or it might be straight 240 volt. The 'works' of the unit are the characteristic curved box on the roof of the RV. The outlets and controls are in a less

deep box on the ceiling of the RV (although, the latest thing is to have the cold air ducted by hidden pipes to outlets, flush with ceiling, at various points in the domestic area).

It is unnecessary to go into detailed instructions here - follow your handbook advice. Two points are made: the demand that an air conditioner puts on the power supply is high; you will find some hook-ups just do not have a big enough amperage to run the conditioner. If it does then be careful about using other appliances at the same time. When it is a bit warm inside but not enough to warrant switching on the air conditioner (or, indeed, the power supply cannot take it) then you can just use the unit's fan. This produces a good refreshing movement of air.

The furnace

Keeping warm is more likely to be the UK requirement and there is a built-in blown hot air system. One system has a control box with a thermometer to show the current temperature in

the RV and a lever to select the desired temperature. There is an on/off control. When this is selected to 'on', a fan in the system blows air through ducting to outlets at various points in the RV - a very welcome one is in the toilet room. Initially cold air will be blown; this is to ensure that there is an air flow through the gas furnace before ignition. After it lights up, warm air will start to flow. The reverse happens when you switch off - the furnace will be closed down but air will still be blown for a minute or so. Understand this cycle otherwise you can be misled into thinking that your furnace is not working.

It is, in fact, a very simple and reliable system - but it uses that precious gas! You will, therefore, undoubtedly invest in some form of electrical heating - a small fan heater which can be switched to a 1kw or 2kw output can be very effective in the sitting part. A particularly useful heater for the bedroom area is a low wattage, background heat type. A typical one is produced by Dimplex and consists of a circular element in a perforated metal container. The useful thing about it is that it has a frost setting and can be a safeguard, during winter storage.

Water heater

Your RV will be generously provided for in this area. One firm (Atwood) seems to have cornered the market with a six US gallon (five Imperial) heater run on gas. The most common models are completely automatic; just select the water heater on at the control panel and it should light - you will hear the roar of the burner flame. If it does not light then a warning light will illuminate. Put the switch to 'off', pause and try again. The only time you are likely to have this difficulty, unless there is a fault, is when there is air in the gas system after storage. This was discussed in Chapter 4. Water temperature control is automatic and pre-set to 'pretty hot' - you cannot adjust this. It takes about 20 minutes for the water to reach this temperature when the burner will switch off; it will then cycle on and off as the temperature falls and is restored.

We have found it something of an extravagance to leave the heater on permanently. We put it on for the 'getting up in the morning' routine. With that complete the heater is turned off and the tankful of hot water is sufficient for casual use during the day. If there is a special need ie washing-up then the heater is put back on for a while - or we boil up an electric kettle full - that 'precious gas and we've paid for the electricity' argument again!

An older style furnace controller with the temperature selector at the top and a thermometer at the bottom.

The latest controllers combine furnace and air conditioner functions.

A small fan heater with a 1kw and 2kw capability is sufficient for all normal RV heating requirements.

The Thetford marine-style toilet has two foot pedals at the front. The left one opens a blade valve which empties the bowl and flushes it, leaving an inch of fresh water in the bottom. If you want to increase this depth of water then operating the right pedal just adds water. All this works very well. The UK element of Thetford are a very good company for after-sales service and they fully support this US product. Check your instruction book to determine which water facilities drain to which waste tanks. A normal set-up is to have the washbasin share the black water tank with the toilet.

The pedals

Water works

Obviously the hot water is supplied to the sinks, washbasin (which, oddly enough, the Americans call a lavatory) and the shower. The latter is a real RV 'goodie'. Full size, it gives a good shower. Setting the water temperature is a small challenge; I find it best to turn the hot and cold fully on and then back off the cold until the water is suitably hot. Very small adjustments are required. I have stuck a small marker on the cold tap which is at the top when the temperature is just right.

Microwave oven

There are few European motorhomes with this luxury. Perhaps it is because of this that there seems to be some bias against them, it often being alleged that the starting load can exceed the capability of a normal hook-up. We have not found this the case although we always take care how many appliances we are using at the same time. Our first Brave had an American microwave; the second one a British one. We have found the latter better

as one can be more certain of the power; we always felt that the 120 volt one was under-powered. Also, the clock on the UK one keeps correct time!

'An awning is as much a foul weather friend as fair.'

Awning

An awning is as much a foul weather friend as fair. It is a considerable asset to be able to keep the area around the door dry during inclement weather. An American awning works under quite a different principle to a European one, resembling a shop blind. It is a very substantial affair and does need handling with some care as it contains a very strong spring. The sequence of its operation is shown in the photographs.

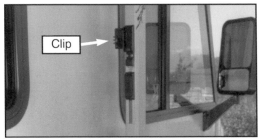

In the stowed position there will be retaining clips, which should be released along with the lever unlocking the wind-in spring. Also loosen off two knobs between the arms and RV wall.

With the rod supplied hooked in the strap loop at the centre of the roll, pull open the canopy.

The arms which were upright will now be horizontal and two narrower stays will be revealed, in a vertical position.

Slide the two vertical stays to be in line with the edge of the canopy and, with them under tension, tighten the knobs, quite positively.

Now raise the two arms to give the required canopy slope.

Awning raising complete!

It is important that you are wary of damage that can be caused by high winds. Also, the canopy should be put on a slope when it is raining so that water is not collected.

Having considered the major appliances, fittings and accessories, it is time to turn to some of the mechanical elements.

Unless the weather is set incredibly fair, I always lower my awning to the maximum down-slope position at night and when leaving the RV for the day. If there is any doubt about the weather outlook then retract the canopy; that is an awful lot of heavy vinyl to have flapping in the wind.

For a journey, you may have to retract your canopy wet - or with leaves stuck to it. Short term this will be OK but always ensure that the canopy is dry and clean for long term storage; mildew and stains can easily form. On a fine day, when long term stored, open the awning as water can creep into the vinyl roll by capillary action.

Engineering matters

Things mechanical are not a strong point of mine - and I have not found this of any disadvantage in American motorhome ownership, which might be of comfort to some of you. Dependability seems to be the byword - backed by regular maintenance. It follows that my technical advice is going to be somewhat simple.

Engine

I have found that all that has required attention from me here is a regular oil and water check. You will find that the dipstick is very long; some care is needed in replacing it in order not to cause it to buckle. There is also a dipstick for the transmission, which is even longer. Read your manual for guidance on a transmission oil check. You will probably find that it should be done with the engine running and after you have exercised the transmission lever through its various selections. The only other 'under bonnet' check is the coolant level which can be judged by looking at the clear portion of the expansion bottle. 'Under bonnet' was used with tongue in cheek. With my first Winnebago, access to the above items was through a 'letter box' at the front. If you want to do any other work on the engine then the large cover inside the motorhome has to be removed.

Routine servicing

Having made light of my maintenance activities, I will emphasise that I do depend on regular workshop servicing.

Your dealer and handbook will advise on the frequency of servicings. The handbook figures will be based on the **normal** use of your commercial base vehicle; typical figures might be a minor servicing eg oil and filter change etc, at 5000 miles with a more major check at 10000. It

Unexpected 'under the bonnet' activity; a blackbird was determined to make the engine compartment its nesting place! The nest had to be removed a number of times.

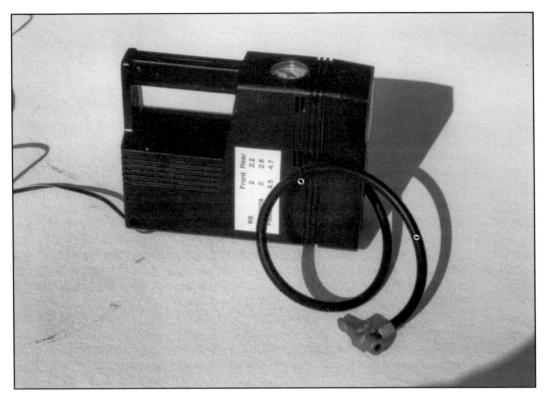

A 12 volt air compressor which is sufficient for 'topping up'. I run it from a 12 volt outlet intended for the bedroom TV. This way it is usng the domestic batteries - which are charged up by the mains. If you use the cigarette lighter then you do not have that advantage.

might take you literally years to reach these mileages but this does not mean that the servicings can have long intervals. With low mileage use then time becomes the criterion - in particular, oil can start breaking down with age. Your dealer will probably suggest that you have a minor service, alternating with a major one, at six monthly intervals, regardless that the mileage has not been covered.

Air pressures

There is a lot you can do to keep your RV fit and healthy. Tyre pressures should be checked. This might not be easy with the double rear wheels where the valves can be difficult to access. You can have extenders fitted and they greatly assist the task. This also applies to air bag suspension assisters. These may be fitted front and rear or just front. They are like rubber bellows and help smooth out the ride and improve the levelness of the motorhome. The pressure at which they should be maintained is a matter of instruction leaflet guidance and experimentation. I have found 60psi to be suitable. One word of caution: when inflating, the pressure rises very much more rapidly than with tyres.

My preparations for a trip include a check of the tyre and air bag pressures. My pressures for all the tyres is 65psi. If you are only used to car or small motorcaravan pressures then this might seem dauntingly high. It is too high for your average pressure gauge and you will have to shop around for an instrument with sufficient range. When it comes to inflating, I have been surprised that a small 12v compressor will do the job. I perhaps should qualify this by saying that I have found that the tyres hold their pressure very well and I have only ever needed to top up, slightly. If some serious inflation was required then such a small device would not prove adequate and a service station facility needed.

On the topic of tyres, I have mentally put aside some money for the summoning of an LGV tyre service company in the event of a puncture. This is using the principle that 'you can't take it (the money) with you'; an entirely reasonable saying to apply, in this case, as I would probably 'go' if I tried to change one of the 34 inch diameter wheels myself!

This prompts thoughts of roadside assistance in general. I can picture the look on the RAC man's face if I was naive enough to think that such a vehicle as an RV, came unconditionally within the terms of membership. You will have to check out the vehicle limits of your rescue organisation.

Carrying a few spares is a good idea. Some suggestions are: Alternator and other engine drive belts. Fuel filter. Bulbs. Fuses.

Permanent extensions to the valve stems make pressure checking and topping up much simpler.

Refuelling

It may seem odd to devote space to the topic of filling up with fuel but, with your special vehicle, some points need consideration. Firstly, you are not going to get to all the pumps that a car uses. Having said that, all such pumps should not be totally dismissed. I personally dislike using LGV pumps; the area can be messy, the pump handles ditto. The rate of delivery can be alarming. My preference is for the larger forecourts of the premier companies. A hot favourite is a supermarket, if one can be sure of the access - when you are putting in 200 litres of diesel then the price advantage can make a lot of difference. This brings up a point on payment. Most filling stations have a credit limit on cards (usually £50). There are ways around this but some discussion is required before you start filling up. The attendant might agree to you making two separate purchases ie put in £50 worth, have the pump reset and then have another £50. Alternatively, it might be that phone authorisation can be obtained for the large credit transaction. Whatever, it can be seen that some negotiation is required. One more point - some pumps have an automatic cut-off at 100 litres. It took me a long time to adopt the following philosophy - having manouevred yourself into a suitable filling station, then fill right up! In the long run it isn't going to cost you any more - and it reduces the number of times that you have to find a suitable place.

Two safety aspects need consideration. Firstly, you should turn off your gas supply at the tank **before** approaching the forecourt. This is the common-sense advice generally offered but I feel that this needs enlargement. It has already been mentioned in the gas refilling situation. A lot of gas can remain in the pipes when the valve is turned off and this would be sufficient to run the fridge, say, for a while. Also, is it a good idea for the fridge to be trying to relight when this gas runs out? Answer - turn off the main

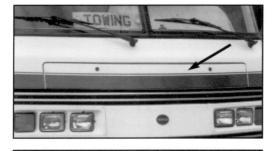

The somewhat restricted access to the forward engine compartment of Winnebago No.1 ...

... which was improved on No.2.

valve **and** the fridge control. (It is assumed that you have followed the instruction of not travelling with the oven pilot light on and that you are not running any other gas devices.)

As an aside, it is worth musing on the different 'gas travelling' UK/US situations. The advice to the Europeans is to travel with the gas turned off, in case of an accident. This 'no gas' situation is possible because European fridges are 3-way ie they can be run on the mains, on the gas or, when the engine is running, on 12 volts from the vehicle alternator. This latter facility is not generally available with American fridges - so the gas stays on. What about the accident situation. It is argued (weakly?) that the European removable gas cylinder and flexible piping could be torn loose in a collision; the permanent nature of the US system is not prone to this. Suffice to say that hundreds of thousands (if not millions) of RVs are travelling the length and breadth of the USA with their gas turned on!

The final point about refuelling - watch out for the height of the filling station's canopy!

Servicing
Much has already been made of regular maintenance and I think that your selection of dealer should be very much governed by this. When considering your purchase, check up on the dealer's workshop facility - you aren't going to

be able to pop into your local garage for diagnosis of a problem with your 6.2 litre Chevrolet diesel, with automatic transmission, say. If you are buying new then the MoT requirement may seem a long way off - but the time **will** come; this is another point to check with your dealer. Strangely, an American motorhome only requires a car-type MoT (Class IV) but, clearly, this cannot be done by a garage with just car facilities. Over to you, Mr Dealer!

I think the key to mechanically trouble-free American motorhome ownership is preparedness to match the sophistication of the vehicle with the cost of its maintenance. A dealership which provides good after-sales service is something to look for here and establishing with them a pattern of preventative servicing.

With the machine all up and running, now is the time to think about some aspects of driving and ownership.

Useful fact?

15mpg = 3.5 miles per litre

```
+-------+---------+--------+--------+--------+-------+-------+
|       |         | AMOUNT | AMOUNT | FUEL   | MPG   |RUNNING|
| DATE  | MILEAGE | LITRES | GALLONS|RUNNING | THIS  | MPG   |
|       |         |        |        | TOTAL  | FILL  |       |
+-------+---------+--------+--------+--------+-------+-------+
| 1993  |         |        |        |        |       |       |
|31 NOV | 1660    |        |        |        |       |       |
|22 DEC | 1983    | 100.20 | 22.02  | 22.02  | 14.67 | 14.67 |
|30 JAN | 2308    | 100.31 | 22.05  | 44.07  | 14.74 | 14.70 |
|08 FEB | 2642    | 122.85 | 27.00  | 71.07  | 12.37 | 13.82 |
|04 APR | 3033    | 134.88 | 29.64  | 100.71 | 13.19 | 13.63 |
|24 APR | 3327    | 100.13 | 22.01  | 122.72 | 13.36 | 13.58 |
|08 MAY | 3761    |  88.57 | 19.47  | 142.18 | 22.30 | 14.78 |
|17 MAY | 4089    |  87.05 | 19.13  | 161.32 | 17.14 | 15.06 |
|25 MAY | 4346    |  99.42 | 21.85  | 183.17 | 11.76 | 14.66 |
|12 JUN | 4893    | 129.42 | 28.44  | 211.61 | 19.23 | 15.28 |
|21 JUN | 5308    | 100.00 | 21.98  | 233.59 | 18.88 | 15.62 |
|02 JUL | 5710    |  82.04 | 18.03  | 251.62 | 22.30 | 16.10 |
|07 JUL | 5935    |  92.72 | 20.38  | 272.00 | 11.04 | 15.72 |
+-------+---------+--------+--------+--------+-------+-------+
```

It is useful and interesting to keep a fuel log - if only to be able to answer the most frequently asked question, 'How many miles to the gallon does that thing do?' This was the early days of Winnebago No.1 and it can be seen that the mpg is improving with time. It eventually settled at a good 16mpg. With a later log I found it useful to add a column 'miles per litre'. This helps with critical refuels.

Driving

Driving a very large vehicle has been touched on, but this is now considered in more detail.

Pre-start checks

This phrase has been borrowed from the flying scene but it is very appropriate to the RV one. You are trusting an awful lot to luck if you just jump into your large vehicle and drive straight off. Be like a good aircraft captain and take that stroll around the outside before start-up. Are all the hatches secure? Here's a seemingly silly question - but it has been done - is the electricity cable disconnected? Door mat stowed - TV aerial down - windows closed - you can add your own items. An RV is not a car and does require some extra thought.

Whilst you are walking around you can formulate some plan for your immediate manoeuvring. If backing up is required then your most useful aid is your partner - never mind mirrors, rear view TV cameras - a human being at the back telling you all is clear will beat the lot. And never mind also the disdainful looks of any onlooking LGV drivers - they probably haven't bought their vehicles!

For its size you will possibly be surprised just how manouevrable an RV is. For instance, whilst the overall length is large, a lot of that can

The open road - Glencoe.

be overhang. The wheelbase is a factor in determining the turning circle. The other thing in your favour is power steering - a few effortless turns of the steering wheel gives you full lock - and a good one at that. Remember that, in an A-class, you are sitting well forward; get a mental picture of where the front wheels are in relation to your seat - pretty well right underneath it. You can afford to drive well up to obstacles and into turns when manoeuvring.

That overhang

The long rear overhang, giving a short wheelbase, may be on your side when it comes to turning circle but there is a snag; remember that it is going to move in the opposite direction to the way that you are turning. What can this possibly mean? Well, picture yourself hard up against a brick wall on your (UK) near-side. Now do a sharp angled pull-out to the right. The vehicle will turn right but the rear will move to the left - and scrape the wall. In this situation, monitor your rear end in the mirrors and adjust your turn accordingly.

On the move

Moving away from your parking place requires engagement of gears and here you have wonderful automatic transmission on your side. If you are at all daunted by the thought of driving an RV then remember that you have this

tremendous facility helping you. A typical situation is coming up to a roundabout - no fiddling about with a gear lever and clutch at the same time as trying to check whether all is clear. Just look and brake or accelerate as required.

With the increase in world travel, many potential RV owners will have experienced automatic transmission. If you haven't, then be assured that it really is simplicity itself. One big thing to remember is to keep your left foot back out of the way - you will only apply the brake with your left foot, thinking that it is the clutch, once. The jolt of your stop should remind you not to do it again. To begin with, tuck the left foot back almost under your seat, as a reminder.

A peculiarity of American vehicles is the parking brake. This is on the left and is foot-operated. Push down on the pedal and it will stay down. There will be a handle to pull to release it. Another braking oddity is that the automatic transmission can be 'braked'. There is a **P** for parked position on the selector and the lever must be placed in this position, when you want to stop the engine. With **P** selected the motorhome should not roll forward or back, in spite of gradient and whether the engine is running or not. Nevertheless, the foot-operated parking brake should be applied when you stop the engine.

Adjusting side mirrors can be a test of marital harmony. Some of this can be eased if you have a way of more or less getting them right and then only requiring the assistance of the 'light touch' for the fine adjustment. First adjust your mirrors very accurately, with the sides, viewed looking into the mirror, vertical. Take a piece of wood about the size and substance of a 12in ruler and place it horizontally across the mirror at some convenient and easily identifiable position. (I was lucky to have the ledge of the smaller mirror on which to rest it.) Move the wood so that one end is touching the window glass. With a pencil laid flat on the glass, mark off the angle at which the wood and glass meet; saw to this line. Replace the wood at the original location but with the angled end now touching the glass; mark off the position of the mirror's vertical edges. Now stick a piece of plastic insulating tape on the window to exactly indicate the place and angle where the glass and wood meet. Label the face of the piece of wood (near or offside). Turn it over and repeat the exercise for the other mirror using the uncut end. If your mirrors are moved then they can be re-adjusted by holding the piece of wood in position and moving them until the end of the wood is aligned with the tape mark.

After , **P** the other positions of the selector lever are:

R	-	**Reverse**
N	-	**Neutral**
Ⓓ	-	**Overdrive**
D	-	**Drive**
2	-	**2nd gear**
1	-	**1st gear**

The automatic transmission indicator. Note the instruction; when in 'Park', applying the foot brake before selecting a gear is not an option - it is an essential. If there is no pressure on the brake pedal you will not be able to move the lever.

Note that this means that you have only four forward gears not the five that is standard, these days, with manual gear changes - though there are some five speed automatic transmissions. The use of these selections will be discussed.

Moving off

With the engine started, put your (right) foot on the brake, select overdrive by moving the automatic transmission lever, with it pulled towards you, and release the parking brake. Transfer your right foot from the brake to the accelerator and apply sufficient power to move away. A previous point made is repeated: if you are on a hill the RV will not roll back when you take your foot off the brake - farewell 'hill starts'! On the move you just accelerate and brake as required. As you proceed, the automatic transmission will select the correct gear depending on a combination of speed, up-gradient and amount of accelerator being applied. It really is that simple. This means that, with normal acceleration on the level, the transmission will change up through the gears as the speed increases; going up a hill, it will change down, gear by gear, as the speed falls. If you wish to accelerate rapidly, typically for overtaking, then doing the natural thing of putting your foot hard down will cause the transmission to change down - or, if you are already in a lower gear, hold you in that - to give better acceleration.

I find that I 'feel' for my engine and transmission so I don't simply sit there with my foot set, or going further down, at gradients. If it is a fair one and you have a lot of throttle set then the change down can seem quite fierce. I sense this might be the case and back off the pedal a bit and allow the speed to drop a little. You might find yourself easing off the pedal also during acceleration, allowing the transmission to change up rather than hold itself in a lower gear. You will get a feel for all this with experience.

Had you wished to reverse initially then **R** would have been selected. On these selections, it is my experience, with the Winnebago, and with hire cars in the USA, that the selector pointer does not settle exactly on the letter. Near enough seems to be good enough.

Further points

We have used overdrive and reverse but what about the other possible selections? **N**, in my experience, is rarely used. It does what is says and selects neutral gear. This could be useful if the engine stalls, on the move, (unlikely with a diesel) and you want to restart without stopping. You could select **N** if there is a hold-up at road works, say, instead of sitting with overdrive selected and your foot on the brake - but it is better to select **P** and be sure that the vehicle will not move.

The rest of the selections are used to overcome the automatics and hold the RV in the gear selected (or a lower one should road conditions demand it):

D - put the lever at **D** if you do not want the transmission to change up into overdrive. With the lever at **D**, the transmission may drop down to 2nd or 1st if, say, a gradient is encountered but, on the level, it will not go into overdrive.

2 - this will hold the transmission at or below 2nd gear. Typical use of this is if you are climbing a fairly long gradient of varying steepness and the automatics get you down to 2nd gear. With overdrive or drive selected the transmis-

sion might change up again as the gradient slackens a bit, only to change back to 2nd when it increases and so on. You will sense that this 'hunting' is not doing the transmission a great deal of good. Selecting **2** will hold it in 2nd gear until the whole gradient has been negotiated.

1 - the same case as for **2** but with a steeper gradient.

Engine braking

If you stay in overdrive then when you go downhill the transmission will remain in that highest gear; therefore, there will be no engine braking. You can obtain this, if the gradient demands it, by selecting **D** (or even **2** or **1** in severe cases). There will be speed limits in your operating manual for selecting these lower gears. Should you be going faster than those, then the gear will not be selected. On the topic of engine braking, there is not the same slowing effect from a diesel engine as a petrol one (that is why large lorries have a vacuum brake - to set up a back pressure in the exhaust manifold to slow the engine and thus the vehicle). This lesser engine braking should be borne in mind when approaching a steep down gradient - lose some of your speed and select the lower gear before you start down, otherwise you will be hammering the brakes.

Shutting down

Before you shut down, move the selector to **P**. If you forget to do this then you will not be able to remove the ignition key until you have selected **P**. If you leave the key in the ignition then you will not be able to restart the engine until you have selected **P**. It can be seen that all this is a safeguard against starting the engine in gear. If you have to leave your seat with the engine running then do a double check that the selector is at **P**. Sounds like a statement of the obvious but the mistake can be made!

Manual

To reassure yourself on all the foregoing then study the operating manual for your vehicle. It can be a bit of a challenge, sifting out the vital stuff from amongst the warnings of serious damage, injury - or instant death!

Cruise control

Given the road systems in the USA - Interstates and the like - and the length of the journeys that

When 'auto' driving, don't disregard your experience with manual gear selection. If you feel that a lower gear is called for, by conditions, then manually select it. I find this particularly applicable when towing a car - which is discussed later.

the Americans undertake, letting the accelerator foot have a bit of a rest is considered a necessity. Hence, you will find cruise control as a standard RV fitting. When you are driving along at your required speed and make a few selections, the system will maintain your speed, regardless of change of gradient etc. There are a number of refinements to this, not the least being that, if you brake then the system will cut out. Your manual will give instructions for operating cruise control. The usefulness of it in this country depends on how often you encounter suitable conditions - and how strong a nerve you have! It is handy, now and then, to allow you to have a bit of stretch but my experience is that, unless you meet unusually quiet motorway conditions, there is fairly frequent adjustment required - or deselection and reselection, leading you to the conclusion that you might as well be using your right foot! Opinion on this will vary from owner to owner.

Other mechanics

Power steering is 'real' power steering and is incredibly light. In fact, this can lead sometimes to over-correcting. I have found, on long straight runs, I am changing the pressure on the steering wheel constantly from left to right to maintain a straight line - but what is happening is that I am interfering with the vehicle's in-built tendency to travel in that straight line anyway. If you find yourself getting into this 'weaving' situation then just relax your grip on the wheel - and look well ahead.

Power steering well and truly comes into its own with manoeuvring, making it incredibly easy.

Lighting control, trafficators, horn and the like are very similar to UK types. A USA convention is to have dashboard switching for the side and headlamps; only main beam dipping is on the control column stalk. Windscreen wiping, with excellent intermittent control and washing, are standard features.

Heating and ventilation

A complaint often levelled at European motorcaravans is that the en route heating can be poor because the converter has not taken account of the fact that the cab heater has to heat a much larger volume than that required in the base vehicle's commercial guise. Not so in the RV. There is the cab heating but in addition you will have a 'rear heater' with high and low settings. This takes engine heat to an exchanger at the rear of the motorhome which is distributed by a fan. It is extremely effective, as is the system for further using engine heat to provide a tankful of hot water at the completion of your journey.

Engine fan

On the topic of engine heat, a noise that will undoubtedly cause alarm when you first hear it is the engine cooling fan coming into operation. Under normal conditions it is stationary or running very slowly; when the water reaches a pre-set temperature it starts a fast rotation under a clutch control. It is quite noisy compared with the normal engine sound but it will soon die gradually away, under that clutch control, as the temperature is lowered. You can seek some reassurance that all is normal by noting the engine temperature at which your fan starts up.

UK mechanical changes

For use on British roads there are a very few modifications required. The only real one is lighting. Something has to be done about the dipping direction of the headlamps - replacement units will probably be fitted. American vehicles do not have separate rear trafficator lights; when you indicate a turn then the appropriate brake light flashes. If you are braking and indicating then the direction of turn brake light will flash and the other one will be steady. So work is required to fit separate orange trafficator lights. It may also be necessary to install a reversing light(s) and a rear red fog lamp(s).

Shortcomings

Can there be anything wanting in this mechanical 'dream machine'? Well - yes! My two Winnebagos have not had a mileage trip meter - which I miss. There is also no clock, a shortcoming easily cured.

Any more comments?

On the mechanical front I have found an RV to be incredibly trouble free and very satisfactory. I do not think that this is just good luck. I believe that it rests on the specification and quality of the base vehicle and on the expectations of the very large and competitive USA market.

It is perhaps invidious to make comparisons but judging from personal experience and that of others, picked up in conversations and articles in magazines, the European motorcaravan market just cannot match the USA one in the quality and dependability area.

More thoughts on driving

It has already been pointed out that an RV is normally at least 8 feet wide - 8ft 6ins ones are on the market. I found an 8 foot width totally terrifying for my 150 mile journey home from the dealer. This reduced to 'disconcerting' for the next few trips. After a few months of ownership, I found it of no consequence! There is the added complication of left-hand drive. Again, like the width, it is just a matter of experience. Most lorries, coaches and buses are 2.5 metres (8ft 3ins) so there is often not a lot of room to spare particularly when you take into account the extra width added by the mirrors. If in doubt slow down and be prepared to stop.

Other factors

The full list of considerations related to the size of an RV:

> Width
> Weight.
> Length.
> Height.
> Body overhang.
> Overtaking performance.
> Stopping distance.
> Power needed to climb uphill.
> Downhill considerations.
> The effect on a large vehicle of rapid changes of speed and direction.

By the way, if you are considering an RV, you need to take into account whether your partner is of a nervous disposition! Sitting calmly in the right-hand seat with no steering wheel, only a few inches from the white line on some of our, so called, 'A' roads, with a 38 tonner coming towards you, does require some grit.

All these factors mean that it requires more skill and common sense to drive a larger vehicle. You may have come across the term 'defensive driving' ie driving with anticipation, good observation and total control; a classic example, often given, is the anticipation of what another driver is going to do before he knows himself! Defensive driving is good practice in an RV.

Height

It is obvious that you can do horrendous damage to your RV if you do not take account of overhead obstructions. Some are obvious and you will notice them eg a car park height barrier. But you will have to start being aware of low bridges, petrol station canopies - and trees! It is a requirement for a commercial vehicle over three metres (10 feet) high to have the height prominently displayed in the driving cab. Why not voluntarily follow this example - and why not add length, width and weight - in Imperial and metric measure.

Turning

There has already been reference to length in the

A thought - why not arrange your first few trips to be on a Sunday when commercial traffic is at a minimum?

It is useful to know that, in the UK, if the height of bridge is unmarked then the clearance is at least five metres (16ft 6ins).

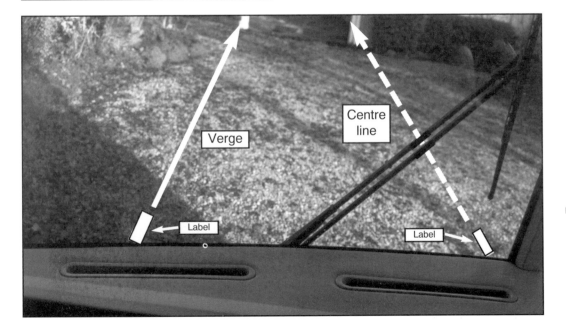

Verge

Centre line

Label

Label

Learning a new position on the road can be greatly assisted with a simple device. I positioned an adhesive address label on the bottom edge of the windscreen, aligned with the verge when viewed from the normal driving position. Just a glance at it, now and then, is most reassuring. Another one for the centre-line of the road is equally useful.

My placard for Winnebago No.1. I didn't take the brochure figures but used a tape measure. For the height I dangled a weighted piece of string from a pole resting on the highest point, the air conditioner, and then measured the length of string. I was pleased that I had gone to this trouble when I found myself having to tackle an 11 foot bridge *en route* to the CC club site at Gowerton, South Wales.

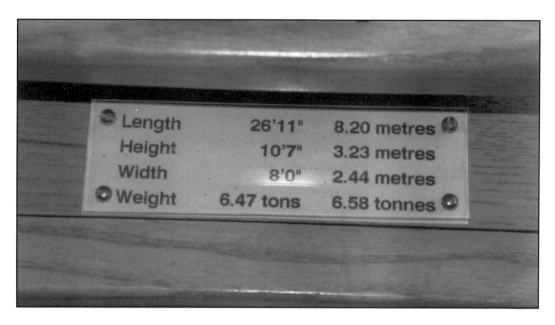

Length	26'11"	8.20 metres	
Height	10'7"	3.23 metres	
Width	8'0"	2.44 metres	
Weight	6.47 tons	6.58 tonnes	

consideration of the effect of rear overhang. The extra length is a factor at roundabouts and sharp road bends which require some care. With the former and right bends you need to make sure you do not 'cut the corners', which is easy to do as they are away from your side of the vehicle.

Rear view mirrors

In a car, mirrors mainly provide information on other traffic. RV mirrors do this as well but they are also essential manoeuvring aids. Fortunately American motorhomes are generally equipped with excellent mirrors. Two-part ones are usual, the upper section being a general view of the road behind; a lower, smaller, convex section provides a useful view lower down and closer to the vehicle. Part of your pre-start check should be that your mirrors are correctly adjusted. You will become a total side mirror person and find that good adjustment is absolutely essential.

To supplement your mirror information, the assistance of the right hand seat person can prove invaluable. A typical example is joining a motorway from a slip road. If there is no one in the passenger seat then take particular care

This does look like a bit of too close, lay-by parking - but the vehicles are all mine! The imminent birth of our tenth grandchild meant that I had to drive solo, towing the small car, with my wife following up in the estate! The RV is a very useful for such an occasion, it becoming a 'Granny Flat' - the older grandchildren call it the 'Grannymobile'.

when joining a major road from a narrowly angled side road. It is very easy (experience!) to think that the view in the mirror is of the major road when it is, in fact, that of the side road that you are on.

Overtaking

Staying with partner assistance, this is going to be particularly useful when considering overtaking. It will not be so much that the other person will be making the decision that it is safe to overtake but that it is OK for you to pull out and assess the situation for yourself. Remember that 'defensive driving' point, a lot of distance is required for a large vehicle with 'less than car' acceleration.

Stately progress

With RV performance, overtaking is not a common requirement - tractors, JCBs and similar are the only likely barrier to your steady progress. There may be many RV drivers who would decry my usual speeds. I keep well within the 50mph on a single carriage road - I always imagine that a particularly large LGV could be coming around the next corner. On the motorway and dual carriageways, 55 is plenty. Even at these modest speeds, progress is steady and fuel consumption at its best - and you are supposed to be travelling for pleasure.

A problem with these speeds is that, inevitably, a queue builds up behind you. It may seem chauvenistic to say it but my advice is, 'Forget it!' Firstly, it is not entirely your fault that it is there - it is the standard of the road and users of such roads should take account of that in their calculation of travelling time. My second point is that there is little that you can do about it, sensibly and safely. If you pull off to let the traffic past then there is the slowing down to do so; then you have to pull back on again, no doubt infuriating another driver. On a long straight road you might try slowing down and signalling left to indicate that you are holding the verge. But I have found that this has its hazards. It takes some drivers so long to realise what you are doing that, by the time they have the message and start to overtake, there is something coming the other way - whose fault would the resulting accident be?

In your early days, when the number of cars bothers you and you are watching closely, you will be surprised how often they all disappear,

being local traffic. A final queue point - a long clear bit of road can show that many people don't want to overtake, anyway. This may be that they are turning off soon, they lack confidence or they are just curious about your vehicle! There is another danger here - the 'nig nog' who pulls out past you and then slows down to have a good look. He's probably riding right in your mirror blind spot.

A philosophy

One should always drive with consideration for other road users but this does not have to extend to executing peculiar manoeuvres which are quite likely to cause misunderstanding and replace inconvenience with an accident.

Finally ...

Whilst there is resistance to classifying RVs as LGVs, they are large vehicles and I have found it very useful to borrow, from the local library, books on LGV and bus/coach driving. LGV mention leads to thoughts of RV legal matters which will be considered next.

A particularly relevant book is published by HMSO for the Driving Standards Agency of the Department of Transport. The title is *The Bus & Coach Driving Manual* and the price, £8.95.

A bit of a tight squeeze, height-wise, at the entrance to a Caravan Club CL in Derbyshire.

Legalities and such

Even though the numbers are increasing, the sight of an American motorhome on the road is not a common one. This appears to be matched by some apparent uncertainty, in official quarters, about licensing matters. There have been a number of changes in recent times and it might seem that there are some anomalies when applying them to the RV scene.

To justify the sub-heading above and provide more detail, here is a fact on taking a Category C licence test. You cannot take the test in a vehicle of less than 10 tonnes MAM. This means that you cannot use your (say) 8 tonne MAM motorhome, probably weighing 7 tonnes, with it not possible to reduce that figure as it is fittings etc.. But a 'normal' test candidate can use a flat bed lorry with a MAM of 10 tonnes, unloaded and only weighing 3 tonnes!!

Weight division

When discussing weight limitations, the figure used is the allowable maximum specified by the manufacturer , most popularly called the gross vehicle weight - see later. It is emphasised that it is **not** the actual weight of the vehicle at a particular time. The official term for the limit is maximum authorised mass (MAM). 3.5 and 7.5 tonnes are key weight figures and a significant date is 1 January 1997. If you passed your driving test before that then you undoubtedly will have had an old Category A licence. Under EC legislation, new categories were introduced and old Category A holders were granted licences in the new categories B, C1, D1, B+E, C1+E and D1+E.

The C1+E 'concession' is an important one for RV owners as it covers many motorhomes towing a car, if required. It does create a difficulty with the larger RVs weighing more than 7.5 tonnes (16,500lbs). Officially, these owners require a Category C licence ie a large goods vehicle one (the old non-articulated HGV licence). Getting up to standard and passing such a test may not be the greatest hurdle; a bigger one could be meeting the somewhat strict medical requirements.

I have to qualify all the foregoing by saying that it is my interpretation of the information provided for me by DVLA. It is not for me to encourage flouting of the law but I will report that many large RV owners ignore or claim no knowledge of these rules. When I was discussing them with one owner, his mock response was, '7.5 tonnes, officer? What rule is that?' He had removed the weight placard from his RV!

It has been said that those of us who passed the driving test before 1 January 1997 were granted these conversions of our Category A licences to B, C1, D1, B+E, C1+E and D1+E. For those taking the test after that date then there are quite

Category B
Motor car or light van with up to eight passenger seats and a maximum weight below 3.5 tonnes.

Category C1
Medium sized goods vehicles between 3.5 and 7.5 tonnes with a trailer up to 750kg.

Category D1
Refers to buses and will be ignored.

Category B+E
Car with trailer ie a motor car or light van with up to eight passenger seats and a maximum weight below 3.5 tonnes with a trailer over 750kg.

Category C1+E
Medium sized goods vehicles with trailer ie vehicles between 3.5 and 7.5 tonnes with a trailer over 750kg - combined weight not more than 8250kg.

stringent rules. Roughly speaking, a test appropriate to each type has to taken, with trailer, if applicable. Before this can be done then a B (car) test must be passed. So, for the next generation of RV owners, things are certainly going to be a bit tougher. One hope is that, in time, the motorcaravan lobby might win some concessions from the powers that be.

Road fund licence

There may be some lobbying over another motorcaravanning/DVLA matter and that concerns road tax - more correctly called vehicle excise duty. A while ago one would have simply said that motorcaravans paid the same road tax as cars. But it has now been declared that a motorcaravan is a 'goods vehicle' because of the 'relevant fittings and loose items being regarded as goods or burden'. The tax for these 'goods vehicles' depends on weight: below 3.5 tonnes they fall into the 'Private/Light Goods' class. The tax for these is the same as for a car - at the time of writing, £150 per annum. Above 3.5 tonnes, providing the vehicle is not used for trade or business, the taxation class is 'Private/Heavy Goods'. As I write, this is £160. Again, I have given you the letter of the law but before you 'volunteer' that extra £10, check your vehicle registration document. Your RV might be registered as 'Private/Light Goods'.

MoT

It might seem to you that there has been something nonsensical about the interpretation of the rules on licences and tax with regard to motorcaravans. This continues into MoT requirements but this time to the advantage of RVs. It might, indeed, seem crazy that an RV, regardless of weight, only requires the same MoT (Class IV) as a car! Clearly, it cannot be carried out by a garage with only car MoT facilities. The advice and assistance of your dealer is going to be very valuable when it comes to MoT time. He will have an understanding with a suitable local MoT testing station.

It could be that, with time, the anomalies of motorcaravan licensing will be resolved. This is where a good dealer can step in - he should be up-to-date with the requirements at the time you are considering purchase.

Insurance

Obviously, like any other road vehicle, an RV must be insured. Equally clearly, insurance companies regard motorhomes in a different light to cars. Because of this, it is as well to deal with a company that understands the market. Approach one that does not and you may get a very strange reaction when you give details, 'The value? Well its £60,000 - and it has a 6.5 litre engine - and is 30 feet long ...' If you're on the phone I would think the line would go a bit quiet! Study the magazines for the adverts of the specialist companies. You might care, like me, to use the insurance facility offered through The Caravan Club. It is these companies who appreciate that, in general, motorhomes are driven (carefully?) by mature drivers - and that the annual mileage is likely to be way below that of a car. For these reasons, whilst you will have to pay more than for a car, you should find that the extra cost of RV insurance is not in relation to the greater, compared with a car, value, size etc.

Speed limits

Requirements change when the 3.5 tonnes boundary is crossed. Below that, car limits apply ie motorway and dual carriageway, 70 mph; other, 60. Above the weight the motorway limit is still 70 but the dual carriageway one drops to 60 mph and the other roads' one, unless otherwise placarded, to 50 mph. If you are towing, the motorway speed drops to 60 ie the three speeds are 60/60/50. These are also the limits for motorcaravans that are longer than 12 metres (39.4 feet).

Weight

Reference was made earlier to the fact that there is a legal requirement for the weight of a vehicle to be kept within the limits prescribed by the manufacturer. This is a real minefield for many owners of European motorcaravans. Firstly those limits are often not readily available and can be lacking in generosity. The payloads of some are unbelievably small. You will not have these problems with an RV. American law is obviously much more demanding in this area and you will find a placard on your vehicle clearly stating the weight limits. These will be repeated in the handbook (see over) together with an explanation of terms and what is and is not included in the given basic weight - a point often lacking in the UK market.

Weight definitions

It is appropriate to consider the different weight terminology used by the Americans. Firstly, the primary unit is the good old pound - but, hopefully,

Speed summary
'Normal' RV motorway/dual carriageway/ other road 70/60/50. Towing or >12m 60/60/50.

Nasty thought! If you don't have the correct licence to drive your RV, is your insurance valid?

Do not confuse metric tonne with our old Imperial tons.
1 tonne = 1000kg
1 ton = 2240lbs
= 1016kg

Weight conversions to keep in mind:

7.5 tonnes is equal to 16,500lbs approximately.

3.5 tonnes 7,700lbs

MOTOR HOME WEIGHT INFORMATION

SERIES NAME __ BRAVE   SERIAL NO. _____ 10F567280051

MODEL _____ 1997 28RC   CHASSIS VIN _____ 1GBKP37FXT3313421

		POUNDS	KGS
GAWR (GROSS AXLE WEIGHT RATING) MEAMS MAXIMUM LOAD CARRIED BY AN AXLE.	FRONT.......	5,500	2,495
	REAR........	10,000	4,536

GVWR (GROSS VEHICLE WEIGHT RATING) _____ **14,800   6,713**
MEANS THE MAXIMUM PERMISSIBLE WEIGHT OF THIS MOTOR HOME. THE GVWR IS EQUAL
TO OR GREATER THAN THE SUM OF THE UNLOADED VEHICLE WEIGHT PLUS THE NET CARRYING
CAPACITY.

***UVW** (UNLOADED VEHICLE WEIGHT)_____ **11,478   5,206**
MEANS THE WEIGHT OF THIS MOTOR HOME AS BUILT AT THE FACTORY WITH FULL FUEL,
ENGINE OIL, AND COOLANTS. THE UVW DOES NOT INCLUDE CARGO, FRESH WATER, LP GAS,
OCCUPANTS, OR DEALER INSTALLED ACCESSORIES.

****NCC** (NET CARRY CAPACITY) _____ **3,322   1,506**
MEANS THE MAXIMUM WEIGHT OF ALL OCCUPANTS INCLUDING THE DRIVER, PERSONAL
BELONGINGS, FOOD, FRESH WATER, LP GAS, TOOLS, TONGUE WEIGHT OF TOWED VEHICLE,
DEALER INSTALLED ACCESSORIES, ETC., THAT CAN BE CARRIED BY THIS MOTOR HOME.
(NCC IS EQUAL TO OR LESS THAN GVWR MINUS UVW.)

*****GCWR** (GROSS COMBINATION WEIGHT RATING) _____ **19,000   8,618**
MEANS THE VALUE SPECIFIED BY THE MOTOR HOME MANUFACTURER AS THE MAXIMUM
ALLOWABLE LOADED WEIGHT OF THIS MOTOR HOME WITH ITS TOWED TRAILER OR TOWED
VEHICLE.

***FACTORY INSTALLED OPTIONS** _____ **597   270**
(WEIGHT DOES NOT INCLUDE CUSTOMIZING OR DEALER INSTALLED.)

THIS MOTOR HOME IS CAPABLE OF CARRYING UP TO __64 GALLONS OF FRESH WATER (INCLUDING WATER HEATER) FOR A TOTAL OF 533
POUNDS, (242 KG), AND 40 GALLONS OF ENGINE FUEL FOR A TOTAL OF 280 POUNDS, (127 KG). REFERENCE: WEIGHT OF FRESH
WATER IS 8.33 LBS./GAL.; WEIGHT OF LP GAS IS 4.5 LBS./GAL. (AVERAGE); ENGINE FUEL IS ___7 LBS. PER GALLON.

* Approximate due to variation of chassis weight and weighing method.

* * NCC may also be referred to as "payload."

* * * If the "trailer" is not equipped with brakes that are activated when the motor home brakes
are applied, the GCWR equals the GVWR plus 1,000 lbs. An exception is any motor home
model for which towing is not permitted. In that case, GCWR equals GVWR. For purposes
of this definition, the "trailer" can be a trailer, a vehicle towed on a dolly, or a vehicle towed
by means of a tow bar.

This weight information is provided for your information and meets the requirements set forth by the Recreation Vehicle Industry Association.

CONSULT OWNER'S MANUAL FOR SPECIFIC WEIGHING
INSTRUCTIONS AND TOWING GUIDELINES.

Remember, motor homes should be operated within recommended gross vehicle weight ratings
(GVWR). For safer operating and handling conditions, you must distribute allowable payload
properly. Consult your operator's manual for loading and weighing information.

04-29-97 / 11:53:40

P. O. Box 152 • 605 West Crystal Lake Road • Forest City, Iowa 50436 • PH: 515/582-3535 • FAX: 515/582-6966

FORM 42SHO (05/13/96) DLC   117396-02D

there will also be kilograms on the comprehensive specification sheet which will come with your motorhome - see example opposite. There will be four stated weight limitations:

Gross axle weight ratings (GAWR) for the front and rear axles, ie the maximum loads that each of these axles should bear. My Winnebago 28RC has 5,500lbs (2,495kgs) for the front and 10,000lbs (4,536kgs) for the rear.

Gross vehicle weight rating (GVWR) ie the maximum total weight to be carried by the chassis - Winnebago, 14,800lbs (6,713kgs). It will be noted that this is less than the total of the front and rear GAWRs but this gives some allowance for nose or tail heaviness.

Gross combined weight rating (GCWR) ie the combined weight of the vehicle plus any pulled load - Winnebago, 19,000lbs (8,618kgs).

Your handbook will also give you the **unloaded vehicle weight** (UVW) of the RV. This can be considered to be the 'leaving the production line' weight ie the vehicle complete and with a full fuel tank but all other tanks and storage spaces empty but factory installed options fitted - 11,478lbs (5,206kgs). If this unloaded vehicle weight (UVW) is subtracted from the gross vehicle weight rating (GVWR) then the result will be the **net carrying capacity** (NCC) - 3,322lbs (1,506kgs) ie the figure that you want, 'How much can I put on board?' The answer is a lot! Part of what you 'put on board' are dealer installed options - with a 'fully loaded' RV these are not likely to amount to much. The weight of a full fresh water tank and of LP gas are provided. These will help you refine the payload figure. If you are an experienced motorcaravanner then you will be able to appreciate the generosity of this - and fullness of the detailing.

If you should require reassurance that you are keeping within these limits then you can take your RV to a public weighbridge. I did this once with my first Winnebago loaded with all the stuff we keep on board (which basically means it was at a weight at which we normally travel, less food and clothes). The result of the weighings was: Front - 4,520lbs; Rear - 7,364lbs; Whole vehicle - 11,663lbs. You might notice that there is a discrepancy in the total - I wasn't on board for the final reading! Note that the front reading is nearer to the maximum

(5,500lbs) than the rear (10,000lbs) but that would figure as it will be the rear one that will increase mostly with more loading. So, with this wealth of information there should be no excuse for being overweight - not that this is a likely event with an RV.

Tyre pressures
Another, not often acknowledged, legal requirement is that the tyre pressures should be in accordance with those stated by the manufacturer. Again this is a very grey area in the UK - which manufacturer? The base vehicle? The converter? The tyre manufacturer? With your RV there is no doubt - the pressures are on the same placard as the weight limitations - 65 psi for the Winnebago.

Storage
Coming under the legal umbrella are thoughts of where you are going to store your RV. If you intend parking it on your property then you need to be sure that there are no restrictions in your deeds that would prohibit such an activity. An awkward neighbour would be quick to point this out. Even if there are no such restrictions, those neighbours could object, particularly about such a large vehicle, and make life difficult. You will know whether this potential problem applies to your situation.

Ready for the off
With everything legally shipshape, it is time to think of the things you need to put on board before you get on the road.

Apart from Ministry of Transport weighbridges there are ones operated by commercial concerns for their own benefit which are also available to the general public - for a fee.

Fitting out

With your RV sitting in the drive or wherever, it is time to think of loading it up for your first trip.

With it being so home-like, many aspects of equipping your motorhome are going to be straightforward. With a European motorcaravan, the amount of payload and space available have to be seriously considered. Whilst there are still constraints in these areas with an RV, they are nowhere near so limiting. We will go through a day's living and the contents of my motorhome to consider the facilities that are available and what to put on board.

The rear corner bed of a Winnebago 27 RC - the RC stands for 'rear corner'. A duvet is in evidence.

Sleeping
For two of you there is going to be that wonderful facility of a full size, interior sprung double bed. It may be an 'island bed' ie you can walk down either side of it, or if space demands it, the bed may be in a corner. Either way, the 'senior' couple on board are going to be comfortable. The normal number of RV berths is six. For the No.2 couple a double bed will probably be formed, rapidly, from the settee - simply lift and pull out the front and the seat and back will fold out and down to produce another full size double bed. Berths 5 and 6 will be a little more modest and formed from the table and cushions of the dinette. This double is probably only suitable for children. If you intend using your RV with a 'crowd' then you will have checked out the adequacy of all these beds. As someone who travels light in the numbers area, I can say that a six berth RV is wonderful for just two!

Bedding is your choice - with the rear double you could use blankets and sheets, if that is your preference. In the winter, we still like using our double sleeping bag, from previous motorcaravanning days. Summertime, a duvet is just right. These latter two would be most suitable for the settee and dinette berths. For your permanent double bed, an electric blanket is a great asset particularly for airing the bed after it has not been used for a while. Add a timer switch for complete evening convenience.

Getting up
Time to savour the generous ablution arrangements of an RV. No struggling with a wrap around plastic curtain and a shower head that is really a washbasin tap. Climb into your full size shower - set your water temperature and, when you temporarily turn the water off, leave the mix set by using the lever on the back of the shower head. With generous bathroom cupboard space we leave many duplicate toiletries on board. I think this is a tremendous element of an American motorhome; you can treat it as your

second home, gradually building up a stock of domestic items so that you are always in a 'nearly ready to go' state the whole time. If you are impressed with the tasteful coordination of the decor then you will want to match this with your additions eg towels.

In any motorhome, space is a valuable commodity and its use will be maximised. So, it can seem a bit of a waste that the shower area is only used for a small part of the day. Utilising the space with removable drying rails for towels and wet clothes will be illustrated later.

Breakfast

Thoughts turn to food, with the first meal of the day. It has been seen that cold storage space is generous. This can also be said for dry goods stowage. It may seem strange but perhaps the only difficulty is that some of the cupboards are too large! They are so vast that it is difficult to stow things conveniently. DIY has not been mentioned yet but here is the first suggestion.

You may find it useful - and easy - to install some extra shelving in these cupboards. I found this particularly handy in the crockery one. MDF board and those plastic right angle joints make construction very simple. For storing packets, tins and the like, vegetable racks are very suitable. Stacking plastic boxes are another idea. Experience will lead you to your own solutions. If not fitted, then convert a drawer into a cutlery one with suitable divisions. Line the bottom of the drawer to cut down rattles when travelling. This is a general point: identify items that will make a noise when you are on the road and take some steps to eliminate it. For some areas, lining with cut up rubber mats is appropriate.

For cupboard shelves you can buy anti-slip material which, as well as keeping things in place when you brake or tackle a roundabout, will act as a noise insulator.

Stowage security

The roundabouts just mentioned will be a test of the security of your stowage. The bang at the first one will reveal the item that you have forgotten. Eliminate the tediousness of checking every likely object by permanent security of some sort. A prime example is a table lamp - is there some way of making it permanently stable?

The day

Be it sun or rain - lazy or active - an RV is a marvellous accommodator of all your leisure requirements. Sun? Carry comfortable outside chairs, a table - you undoubtedly have a fitted awning (canopy) to sit under. For the glorious sunny days, have a small barbecue tucked away somewhere. The cook might enjoy the facility of a camping-type cooker to use outside rather than

Breakfast outside, at a CL (see later), with a collection of the paraphernalia that one can carry! Centre are the lightweight chairs and bottom left the very substantial lounging ones. A sun umbrella completes the scene - and the towels are drying in the sun on a clothes airer.

endure the heat of cooking inside. You can run one from the Extend-A-Stay device mentioned in Chapter 4, RV Gas, though this is perhaps a bit over the top; I use the largest, but relatively small, Camping Gaz bottle. As well as our comfortable lounging chairs, we have two lightweight ones which are ideal for breakfast, or whatever, outside. Rain? Time for indoor activities - take your hobbies with you. Perhaps, as I continue with what must begin to seem an excessive list, you will begin to appreciate the immense storage and carrying capacity of an American motorhome!

... take your hobbies (or work even!) with you.

Other items

To continue to add to the list, I will itemise the other contents of my motorhome. One cupboard has pots, pans and other cooking equipment. We have gradually built up a permanent set of such items so they, well and truly, stay on board. Crockery is also duplicated. Two cupboards are allocated to books, both for leisure and reference eg guide books, Good Pub Guide(!), etc. Within a forward cupboard is a power point and it is here that a rechargeable torch is permanently located. It was suggested in the chapter on engineering that you carry some spares. These, and other rarely used items need not clutter up your cupboards or outside lockers. You will find numerous 'cubby holes' in your RV and these can be utilised. Below one of my dinette seats there is a space which is only accessible when you remove the cushions and the wooden seat base. This is ideal for a spare fuel filter, alternator and other drive belts and the like. It is here, also, that I have gathered the emergency equipment: jack, wheel nut spanner, red warning triangles, rope etc. Other 'maybe' items have been squirrelled away over the years. In another 'cubby hole' I have my electrical spares: fuses, bulbs etc.

To an RV, there is little that need be, or indeed can be, added furniture or fittings-wise- it is a complete home. Perhaps a concern might be to protect what is there. We did go for covers to protect the seating in our first Winnebago and then sold it with the fabric looking brand new. With the second we have decide to enjoy the uncluttered furnishings ourselves; the fabrics are extremely durable. We cannot feel as ruthless about the floor coverings; with so much stepping directly in from the outside, the fitted carpet would soon become very tired looking. Loose mats do not look out of place if colours are carefully chosen. One menace to overcome is their movement - carpet creep. You will be aware of the material that you can purchase to prevent this. I found that this was not totally effective until I taped it, around the edges, to the back of the loose pieces. It really does stay put then.

Before moving outside there are two more items to consider and they concern the vital area of safety: hanging inside a cupboard door, adjacent to the cooker, is a fire blanket and, located in an obvious place, a first aid kit.

Those outside lockers
When you were first shown around an RV then the size of the lockers around the outside probably drew a gasp! They are substantial and a tremendous asset. My biggest one is at the rear, below the double bed. It contains those comfortable chairs and the outside table. I have numerous small items contained in three stacked plastic boxes. Later there will be a discussion on locating yourself on a pitch. It might seem prudent, at times, to have the wheels on boards; cut from one inch marine ply, four of these are stored in this rear locker. With covering every eventuality in mind, I have a spade. The hose box I have mentioned is in this locker.

Forward of the large locker is a much smaller one and I regard this as my 'damp' locker (although I do try to keep it aired and dried as much as possible). In it are two buckets - square ones for convenient stowage - containing cleaning cloths and materials and the toilet fluid containers - always have a spare! A pair of RVing wellington boots is a good idea. When travelling, in this locker goes the outside plastic AstroTurf doormat, in a plastic bag. The last locker on the off-side is a small one, again and contains my various lengths of hook-up cable

and spare hose. These are stored in old wire baskets rescued from a discarded deep freeze! Spare engine oil is also carried here.

Moving to the near-side there is just one storage locker and this is large. It is big enough to take a 13kg propane Calor Gas bottle in an upright position, my tool box and the four wedges (see levelling later) I always carry. There is no sacrifice with what you have on board; the aforementioned tool box is my regular one from my workshop - it all comes with me, just in case! I also have a folding step intended for a caravan. You have the great facility of an electric step and this is sufficient for most 'comfortably getting on board' situations. However, there can be circumstances where the climb up that first step can be high. This particularly occurs when you are using wedges on the off-side to level the RV (again, see levelling later). Out comes the locker-stored folding step.

Those other doors
There are other hatches whose doors match those of the lockers and these conceal the permanent gas cylinder, the generator and the waste system dump valves.

Where?
A lot of space has been given to various RV matters but without the 'dream machine' moving one inch! Time to consider some suggestions of where you can go to stay.

The huge rear locker in the 28RC. There is more than room for those big outside chairs, stacking plastic storage boxes - and a barrel!

Sites for your RV

It has been pointed out that this is very much advice from personal experience. This continues here when it comes to choosing places to stay.

Site for free?

Before discussing sites, we can get out of the way the topic of not using them at all. One of the images that motorcaravanning projects, to the man in the street, is that you are completely self-contained (true) and therefore you can just pull up anywhere and stay - known in the business as 'wild camping'. The Americans have a wonderful term - 'boon docking'. Well, in the remoter parts of America and some of our, few and far between, completely wild spots, you may be able to wild camp - but as a general rule it is not on. You need permission to stop on private land and in the UK all land belongs to someone. You will be aware of notices prohibiting such overnight stopping. The absence of notices does not mean that you will not have a landowner, or the police even, chasing you off. There is also the security aspect - even a small motorcaravan, being strange to the area, will attract attention. Think what an RV will do - and that attention could be distinctly undesirable. My advice is, 'Don't wild camp!' Some seasoned RVers will tell you otherwise; their nerves must be stronger than mine - and skins thicker!

Sites proper

So we are looking for camp sites - I think this sounds such an unattractive term, only to be beaten by caravan site - the mental picture is wrong. The US 'campground' has a better ring. I am going to heartily recommend to you the facilities of The Caravan Club. As its title implies, it was established for the benefit of caravanners but now, unreservedly, accepts motorcaravanners.

Founded in 1907, The Caravan Club has provided Club Sites and other amenities for many years and now its 285,000 members enjoy a nationwide network of some 200 of these sites. They are modern and well equipped with over

80% of pitches having their own electric hook-up points and a full facility block, including laundry room, on most sites. Over half of them also have facilities for the disabled.

What is important to us is that these Club Sites usually have the capacity and willingness to accept American motorhomes. With your large, heavy vehicle, you are going to be looking for an adequate approach road and entrance, roads on the site and, for the average UK weather picture, a hardstanding pitch or very firm grass. Whilst you can survive without electricity, given a choice you would prefer to have it. Also you can manage with your own toilet facilities but the use of a modern, well furnished toilet block might be useful, especially if it is equipped with a laundry room and dishwashing section. Either at the beginning or end of your stay you would like the use of a 'dumping station' and fresh water refill point.

All these conveniences are offered by those attractively located and well maintained Club Sites of The Caravan Club. Add to the list above the courtesy and efficiency of the warden and his staff and the generally good and considerate behaviour of your fellow 'campers' and you have an excellent 'camping' situation.

The Caravan Club logo has been incorporated into rather grand gates to the new Club Site at Edinburgh.

Membership and site fees

There is a fee to join The Caravan Club, currently £5. The annual subscription is £27.50. The joining fee is waived if payment is by credit card continuous payment or direct debit. This subscription allows you to use member-only sites. (At sites that admit non-members, you pay £4 per night less than the casual user.) You receive a very comprehensive sites directory once every two years (with an up-date in the intervening year) and eight issues a year of the members' magazine. The Club offers a large range of services to members - travel, insurance, loans and a line of accessories.

Fees for your stop vary with season, location and facilities on the site. Two examples at the top and bottom of the range are given below.

A quiet corner at The Caravan Club Site near Carlisle. This is one of the few Club Sites without toilet block facilities - which, of course, is totally acceptable for the RV scene.

For two adults using electricity:

Highest (typically a popular, fully equipped site on a bank holiday)
£12.25 per night.

Lowest (small remote site in Scotland with minimum facilities, low season)
£6.25 per night.

Charges for children vary between £1.20 and 50p each.

The Doune Club Site is located in an old walled garden.

The Caravan Club have made a special effort to accommodate motorcaravans. Most sites have a ground level waste water facility. Some sites have pitches with dedicated water taps and sewage disposal points.

There is no extra charge for the size of vehicle or for the use of a hardstanding. All members are advised to pre-book for bank holidays and weekends but you would be very wise, on **all** occasions, to ring in advance to see if the site can accommodate your larger outfit.

Other sites

In addition to over 200 of these Club Sites, The Caravan Club Sites Directory also lists over 3000 small sites - informal ones that have been 'certificated' by the Club to meet planning regulations. These Certificated Locations (CLs), as they are known, are for members of the club only and are allowed to accommodate a maximum of five units at any one time, the maximum individual stay being 28 days. A typical CL would be a farmer's field although there are ones in orchards, walled gardens, beside pubs etc. The use of a CL by an RV requires some planning. There will be a part of a typical UK year where the state of the ground will preclude the use of grass by an American motorhome - but there are CLs that offer hardstandings. Whilst generally a CL will have a 12 feet wide access, the approach to and from it may not be suitable for a large vehicle. The answer is to telephone. We have generally found that we are not the first RV enquiry and the owner can quickly offer advice on suitability.

If electricity becomes essential to your RV lifestyle then this need not rule out CL use - there are quite a number with hook-ups and these are listed in the sites book. To be 'certificated' the CL owner has to offer a fresh water supply, rubbish disposal and a chemical toilet disposal point. It might be that the latter is not suitable for RV dumping and some alternative is required; that wheeled tank previously mentioned?

A CL on a farm at Martin, near Cranborne.

If you want a quiet, get away from it all, situation then a CL will be likely to fit your bill. If you prefer a little more action then ...

Commercial sites

The uses of The Caravan Club Sites Directory are not at an end. There is a section on commercial sites. Details can also be found in many caravan site books available in bookshops. These sites are, as their name implies, run as a business and aimed more, perhaps, at the annual holidaymaker. This leads to them possibly having, in addition to water, toilet and electricity facilities, swimming pools, bars, restaurants and the many other things that many people associate with a family holiday. The standards of these sites vary tremendously and it will be for you to decide which ones, if any, are for you.

Another club

The Caravan Club is not alone in providing club-type facilities for the recreationally nomadic. The Camping and Caravanning Club is a similar organisation. However, they have a length limit on motorcaravans of 25 feet which disqualifies the vast majority of RVs.

You might sense that I have some considerable enthusiasm for The Caravan Club - you would be right! So, please, do not spoil things for RVers. Do ring ahead and see if you can be accommodated; take care when you are manoeuvring - look out for the precious grass.

RV outside the UK

The title of this book should preclude mention of Continental use but that would be ignoring the activities of a large number of RV owners. As well as normal summer touring, many take off for winter sunshine to Portugal and the like. This brings thoughts of ferry (and EuroTunnel) use. The Caravan Club Travel Service will be able to help you here. Your size is obviously going to be a financial disadvantage as the companies charge per metre for above a specified length of outfit and there may be a surcharge for height.

Below, provided by The Caravan Club Travel Service, are some sample return fare prices, valid at the time of writing, for a motorhome with a length of 32 feet, and 10ft 6ins high, on typical routes.

> It can be extremely useful if your dealer is able to offer overnight accommodation for your RV when servicing is required.

Sample return ferry fares

Dover to Calais £200 - £300

Portsmouth to Caen £220 - £326

Harwich to Hook of Holland £210 - £350

Plymouth to Santander £502 - £625 + cabin cost

For comparison, an average return fare using the Channel Tunnel is £170 to £230

Ireland is highly recommended by many for motorcaravanning but the ferry fare is a bit of a stumbling block: Fishguard to Rosslare is £400 to £500.

These prices are only samples for 1998. Use The Caravan Club Travel Service facility to check for advice on your best route and any special offers.

> Propane gas might seem a Continental challenge but bulk supplies are available. An adaptor is required. I think it is a classic for Extend-A-Stay and a spare cylinder. You might last your whole trip with this.

A past volume of The Caravan Club Continental Sites Guide and Handbook is to the right. The other overseas travel items are a 'green card', a GB sticker and a camping carnet. Full details of all these items are contained in 'The Motorcaravan Handbook'.

A bit of a tight squeeze into Campingplatz Eggewald, near Horn, Northern Germany.

On the ferry

When you are travelling on a ferry be prepared for discrimination! Not unfair - you are clearly not a car, or a car with a caravan - but you are also not a lorry! I would estimate that 95% of ferry traffic is in the car or lorry bracket so you are the odd one out - and your treatment will match that. We have found that we have always been selected for particular handling, being directed to a special pre-boarding spot. This has generally meant that we have been boarded first, right at the front - or the very last! Remember to pack your patience!

With the size of your RV, it is as well to be personally aware of any height hazards - the ferry crewmen do not have a financial interest in your vehicle - you do. Size is also a thing to watch for when you are negotiating the boarding and disembarking ramp. Remember your rear overhang.

Continental sites

Having safely disembarked, where to stay? Turn to The Caravan Club once more! They publish a Continental Sites Guide and Handbook (in two volumes). As well as offering useful information on each country, it lists hundreds of sites. The entries are composed from contributions of members and their descriptions enable you to decide whether it is the type of site for you. Be aware that 89% of the members of The Caravan Club are caravanners so they did not have the size of an RV in mind when they submitted their reports; so you might find some of the sites not suitable. That aside, the books are invaluable. Volume 1 covers France, Spain, Portugal, Andorra and Morocco; Volume 2 Austria, Benelux, Cyprus, Eastern Europe, Germany, Greece, Italy, Scandinavia and Switzerland.

Finally ...

Before returning to the UK scene, it is mentioned that a number of people use their RV full-time mostly on the Continent. They have sold up their homes and taken to the road. I must say I rather envy their spirit but such a decision does need some careful consideration. As with many other RV matters, you will find the experience of such RVers described in magazines which will give you some feel as to whether it is the way of life for you.

We leave such esoteric RV uses and return to the UK and consider some aspects of settling into your chosen site.

Back in the UK we return to a Caravan Club Site - at Gowerton in South Wales. Note that it is all grass - and this was December! The site was built on ground which was recovered from dismantled steel-works - and it is hard! The nearby site at Pembrey has similarly firm grass. It is only with the ressurance of the warden that I would venture on to such a pitch.

Settling in

It is timely, once more, to point out to those readers who are completely new to motorcaravanning that the fundamentals are covered in *'The Motorcaravan Handbook'* which provides useful information, for the novice, on the use of sites.

A 'room with a view': loch-side at The Caravan Club Site at Onich in the Western Highlands.

Arrival

At the site office there will be a discussion about which pitch you should use. No doubt the warden or proprietor will have in mind ones that are more suitable for larger outfits. At busy times one of these will be allocated - at quieter ones you might be invited to walk around and take your pick! As a general rule (unless the grass areas are exceptionally firm), hardstandings will be used.

Privacy

We have found that, with our larger vehicle, the best thing to do is get away in a corner somewhere, if possible. Nearness to the toilet block is not a consideration; it certainly pays not to be on one of the routes to it. All this retreat is to avoid stares! One thing that you will experience is a lot of interest in your vehicle - in Germany, we had people come right up to the window and cup their hands to the glass to see inside - with us in there!

Positioning

With a spot selected, it is time to drive on - don't forget to think about any dumping and/or water replenishment first. You might be advised by the staff that there is a convention for positioning on the pitch - The Caravan Club had such a rule but this has now been largely abandoned. Convention or not, a caravan will generally be reversed on to its slot for two reasons: it is the only real way to manoeuvre it and, secondly, if everybody does that then you do not have doorways facing each other, which increases privacy. If you wish to conform to this, which is a good idea, then you need to drive in forwards - which is a bonus! For correct spacing, again the old convention was for a caravan to have its rear off-side corner against the pitch number peg. In spite of The Caravan Club having abandoned enforcement of position on a pitch, most members still conform to the old way - it worked! So if you want to follow suit, in addition to going in forward, you should position your front nearside corner against the peg.

Do drive on carefully; with your manoeuvrability it should be possible to avoid going on the grass.

Levelling

Motorcaravanners have to come to terms with levelling - if you don't do so then it is a nuisance. It can seem that an RV is quite a size to get level but it really is no more difficult than with smaller brethren. The principle is the same - you have to raise, somehow, the lower wheels. Which ones these are can be determined with a spirit level. The most convenient sort is a circular one which gives fore and aft and side-to-side

information at the same time. The question arises as to whether the surface on which you are going to place your spirit level is 'level' in relation to the whole of the RV. A good check is to use the floor of the fridge; this should have been installed level for efficient operation. Check the position of the bubble when in the fridge and then compare that with the one when the spirit level is on a surface handy to the driver. With some experimentation a satisfactory location can usually be found.

The usual way of raising the low wheels of a motorcaravan is to use wedges. For an RV these have to be big wedges but you have a big motorcaravan in which to carry them. I have four, cut from solid oak - four are necessary to meet the need to raise both the twin rear wheels; it might be argued that you really need five to cover every eventuality, but I think this is a bit over the top - if things are that bad, move!!

Always arrange the wedges so that you are driving 'downhill' on to them. One difficulty you may find with the automatic transmission is that, having 'climbed' the wedge and gained the necessary height, you lose some of this precious commodity when you put the transmission lever to park, apply the parking brake and release the foot brake. The vehicle rolls back ever so slightly but on the wedges this can be a precious inch. I have found that chocks behind the wheels is the answer. Having driven up the wedges, until

I have found that, on two occasions, the circular spirit level that I am recommending came with the fridge. Check inside before shopping!

To the left is the circular spirit level. Below, 'a wedge' in use. Also in the photo is the rear chock which I recommend and one of my marine ply boards. This wedging situation was on grass and it seemed prudent to guard against sinking in.

One inch thick marine ply board.

level, I hold the RV on the foot brake whilst my wife places the chocks. She comes to the window to tell me that they are in position - that way I know that her fingers are well and truly clear - and I select P, apply the parking brake, and release the foot brake. There is no discernible movement. Apart from preventing the rolling back, I think the chocks also perform a good safety function.

As you drive up the wedges you will be glancing at your spirit level to see when you have achieved sufficient 'lift'. Later, when you examine the situation outside you will be surprised that the amount that the wheels have been raised is quite small. This has led me to 'cheating' now and again. If the surface is suitable eg gravel and the level adjustment required is small then it might be sufficient to scrape away some of the surface material in front of the appropriate wheels and drive into the dips. This technique can be applied to the wedge case to increase the effectiveness of their lift. Don't forget to replace the gravel, or whatever, when you leave!

Obtaining 'drop' instead of, or as well as, 'rise' with a little gravel digging.

Even on totally level ground you might find the step up to the electric step close to comfortable limits, height-wise. Your 'wedging' could well have increased this step height. I have found a folding step, obtainable from caravan accessory shops, very useful.

When it comes time to move off, it might be that the chocks behind the wheels are jammed. Partner's help is called for again. Whilst I 'drive' the vehicle a little further up the wedges, she pulls out the chocks. It is wise, once again, to be aware of the danger to fingers and I have

rope handles attached to the chocks. I also have them on the heavy wedges to help with handling. (Can you guess that I spent a lifetime as a pilot?!)

Doing it in style!
Some RVs are fitted with a jacking system to lift the vehicle to the level position.

Final touches
With the RV level, it's door mat out - electricity cable connected - and that's about it! Just fiddly bits to do, like tuning the television. TV and the motorcaravanner is exhaustively covered in '*The Motorcaravan Handbook*'. To write this, I studied TV reception fairly deeply, realising, amongst other things, the significance of aerial type and orientation. Having acquired this knowledge, I am amazed that the American aerial on an RV works at all, let alone give, most of the time, a very good picture. Its shape bears no resemblance to the UK models; perhaps it is the height to which you can raise the aerial and the quality of the booster system that does the trick. Whatever, you will be mostly very satisfied with the performance of your aerial.

There is one situation where the picture can be poor; this is when the TV signal is vertically polarised. What can this mean? Country-wide, study house TV aerials and you will find that 95% of them lie with their elements in the horizontal plane - then you go to a particular area and the elements are vertical. This indicates that the signal is coming from a relay station (vertically polarised signal) as opposed to a main transmitter (horizontal polarisation). Your RV aerial lies in a horizontal plane and will not be

These two photographs illustrate horizontal and vertical polarisation. Use the 'Image' brand name for orientation. In the top picture the aerial elements are horizontal for a signal from a horizontally polarised signal from a main transmitter. The lower photograph show vertical polarisation usually associated with a relay station.

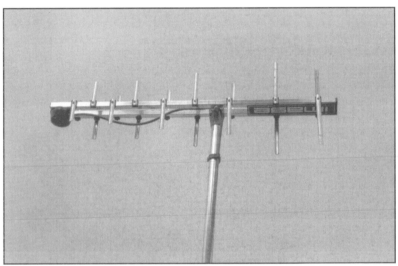

Before lowering the aerial, it should be rotated until these two triangular pieces are lined up to ensure that the aerial is going to lie in the correct position on the roof.

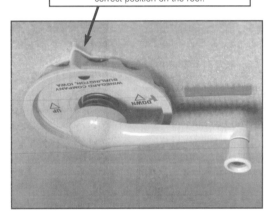

The ceiling mounted, interior control for the TV aerial. Thirteen winds on the handle raises the aerial fully - it should always be fully extended. When it is in the raised position it can be rotated.

too hot at picking up a vertical signal. I have found two solutions to this. The first was possible with Winnebago No.1 because I had my TV free-standing when on site and I could get to the built-in telescopic aerial. The combination of the relay station's vertical signal and it being strong might mean that this gives a better picture than the RV aerial. Another solution is to carry a normal aerial (a universal one stocked by caravan accessory shops) and rig it up outside (the external ladder is useful for this) plugged into the exterior TV socket. You will find this somewhere on your RV - probably in the electric hook-up compartment. This facility is provided with US campgrounds in mind where the hook-ups include cable TV! Mind you, you will come across some Caravan Club Sites where the TV signal is poor and a communal aerial, with a boosted signal, has been set up and there are connections to it on each pitch. If you use the external TV point then you will have to do some switching on the box associated with the TV aerial. Typical markings are ANT AUX VCR. The first is the main aerial and AUX is the external socket.

You do have the wonderful convenience of being able to raise and rotate the regular aerial from within the RV. As one of the easiest clues as to which way to point the aerial, for 'starters', is from nearby houses, I found it convenient to put an arrow on the inside rotation knob to show me which way the aerial was pointing - the direction in which it leans points to the 'front' of the aerial. Having tuned the TV set, small adjustments can then be made to direction to get the best picture.

American TVs do not work in this country which is a pity because RVs come, in the USA,

I have to make an RV criticism! I have found the position of the TVs, literally, a pain in the neck. No.1 I adapted so that it could be taken out of its high stowage and put on a small table when on site. No.2 is not quite so high and has survived modification so far - but perhaps the time will come.

A communal aerial bollard at a Caravan Club Site.

with some nice looking sets. Yours will probably have an empty hole for you to fill with a UK one. Can I suggest that you get one that is 12 volt as well as mains, can operate to all the international standards and has the ability to be retuned by selecting channel numbers, as well as the normal search facility. You can obtain a list of the channels that the various transmitters use for BBC1, BBC2 etc and it makes the setting up of your TV, at a new location, so much easier.

Radio

Thoughts turn from TV to radio. I have found the US radios fitted to my Winnebagos to have excellent performance. I did have a difficulty with the first one in that the illuminated display failed; this was replaced by the dealer and the same thing happened to the second one. I mused on the fact that the reason could be under my control. There is the useful facility of being able to supply the radio from the vehicle battery, when on the move, or the domestic batteries when the ignition is off. I think the mistake I made was to leave the controlling switch to the domestic batteries position when the RV was not in use. Having the display illuminated for that length of time is not a 'natural' thing. Now, when I turn the radio off, I move the switch to the vehicle battery position.

I can't help but slip in my radio tuning tip, although it is not confined to RVs. If you have a favourite station, say Radio 2 then you will know that it broadcasts on frequencies within a particular band - 88 to 91 FM for Radio 2. When you are on the move, the radio will need retuning

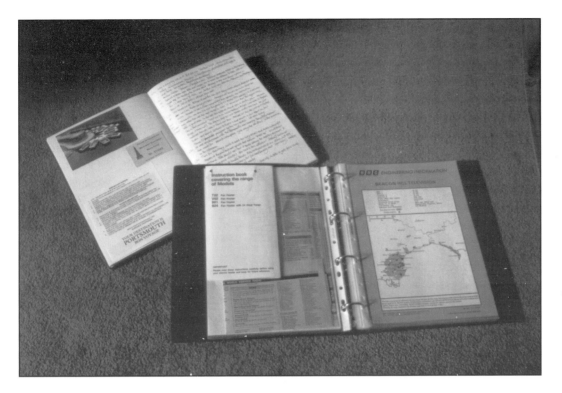

The bottom right book is my 'TV' one. The right hand page is one of the maps produced by the BBC Engineering Department showing the signal coverage of one of the main transmitters. The department is usually asked for single copies of a map of one particular area. This they supply, free of charge, to the senders of a SAE. If you require the full set then there is a charge. See appendix for address. The top left book is my motor-caravan log. I am on my seventh volume now! Apart from keeping a narrative of day to day activities, with photographs, I also record fuel purchases, and the like, for future reference.

- you punch the search button and it stops at all the good reception stations (local commercial ones?) before reaching your Radio 2 one.

Tip: into one of your pre-tune positions save the lowest frequency of the band in which your preferred station broadcasts (88.0 FM for Radio 2). Now, when you want to retune, you select the button giving you 88 and then search - bingo!

Your preferred listening straight away!

Settled in

You will be amazed how quickly you accomplish the few tasks necessary to set yourself up. With those completed, now is the time to think about enjoying your new locale. To do this there is the essential matter of how you are going to get about - and that is considered next.

A tip slipped in! I found that the cupboard that would be handy for stowing a washing-up bucket did not have enough height. So a suitable size plastic stacking box was obtained and rope handles added.

Getting about

An RV is a large vehicle - a 'living' advantage but a 'mobility' disadvantage. In this chapter the topic of 'on site' transport is considered.

In '*The Motorcaravan Handbook*' I have suggested that one way of compensating for possible lack of mobility, with a large European motorcaravan, when on site, is to do some sightseeing on the way and move fairly frequently. With an RV this is hardly practicable. On your journey you are going to have stops but they will really only be roadside ones; all you hope is that you can pick scenic places and be able to pull well away from the road. All this fits in with thoughts on choice of route. Your priority is going to be the most straightforward and safest. This inevitably means that you will use motorways and major roads for most of your journey; the 'get away from it all' can come when you are settled at your destination.

Settled in
With your settling in accomplished, it will be time to muse on the local area. What you are going to be able to do and see is going to depend on your secondary means of transport.

Shanks' Pony
It has been my belief that motorcaravanning and walking are a great combination so if you are in a suitable area, and energetic enough, then there is no need for additional means of transport. This greatly simplifies the organisation of your journey - and is good for you!

Two wheels
Having said that, there are many situations where you will find it incredibly inconvenient and limiting having to walk everywhere, so the next rung up the transport ladder is the bicycle on a rear rack. Motorcaravanners with small vehicles should seriously consider the weight

Shanks' Pony can take you to some interesting spots - Neptune's Staircase near Fort William.

factor with carrying bicycles; an RVer has no such problem. The only thing to bear in mind is an increase in length (shipping length for calculation of ferry fare?).

All the RVs I have come across have a towing facility as standard. This consists of a, bolted to the chassis, construction which carries a square 1½ x 1½ inch hole - a receptor. Into this can be slotted a hollow, square section length of metal, to which a vertical plate is welded and this carries the tow ball. This means that the simplest way of fitting a bike rack to an RV is to purchase one that is intended to be fitted on a tow ball. If you then have one dedicated to the bike rack, the whole thing can be removed and refitted in seconds. It is very secure - and no body drilling is involved. Check that the rack plus bicycles do not obscure the number plate or rear lights. Some of these tow ball racks come with their own plate and lights.

Two wheels plus engine

Many RVers carry a motorcycle. Obviously the rack and its fitting has to be more complex and substantial than that for a bike. Manoeuvring a heavy motorbike could be a problem but this can be greatly assisted with the fitting of a ramp as part of the construction of the rack itself.

Square section going into receptor

Tow ball

Wheel holder for second bike

Excellent cycle tracks in Germany and Austria help the two wheel getting about.

The tow ball mounted type bike rack - with its own lights and number plate.

What cannot be appreciated, in black and white, is the colour coordination! The blue of the car tones with the decal stripes.

Four wheels!

The ultimate transport companion for an RV is a small car; go to the States and you will see that 80% or more of the motorhomes are towing a car. Because it is unusual in this country then it can be regarded with some unwarranted suspicion. Having now towed a car for over six years, I can say that there really is no great problem.

Towing ways

There are three methods of towing. The one that is least contentious, legally, is to have the car on a trailer. This point is made as there can be some

Friends of ours, with a UK Foster & Day motorcaravan, favour the trailer way with decal coordinated car!

debate about the legality of other towing methods. With the car on the trailer, one is clearly just towing a trailer and providing it meets trailer legal requirements then all is well. From my biased point of view, this is where any advantage ends. I briefly tried this method and found it extremely cumbersome. The RV has to be positioned where it can accept the trailer; this has to be manoeuvred on to the towing hitch (a substantial enough trailer to take a car can be incredibly heavy). Ramps have to be put in place and the car driven on (alarming process!) and then it has to be very positively secured. At the end of the journey the reverse process is required - and the trailer parked somewhere. A point of some consequence is the combined weight of the car **and the trailer**. The nose weight of the trailer must be within the limits for the towing hitch. This method is not for me.

A dolly

When garages are recovering broken down vehicles then the normal way is to have the front wheels supported on a two wheel car dolly. This, again, is not a way I favour. There is some question about the legality of this when used for recreational towing as opposed to garage work. It is a requirement that a 'trailer' which weighs more than 750kg (and all but the very smallest cars do) should have brakes fitted to all wheels. In the dolly situation, **its** wheels are braked but the rear wheels of car are not. On the convenience front, much of the awkwardness of the trailer scene applies to the dolly. Having said that, it is a very common USA method - but the market there does mean that dollies tailored for the RV market are readily available. The US car travels in a relatively level position; our dollies put the car up at quite an angle. Their popularity in the USA is also influenced by the fact that it is the only method of towing a car with automatic transmission, unless some modifications are done - or it is one of the (sole?) USA models that allows towing. I see little in this method of towing to appeal.

Dinghy towing

Dinghy towing? I thought we were talking about car towing! 'Dinghy towing' is the American term for towing a car on its own four wheels and this is the method I have used for these many years. A horizontal bracket with two lugs, 2 - 3 feet apart, is engineered on to the front number

Attachment point for foot brake cable

Lugs have rubber caps for non-towing situation

plate area of the car. A frame, either the shape of an 'A' or a 'Y' is attached to the lugs - by the feet of the 'A' or the two tops of the 'Y'. (The 'Y' shape has the advantage that it can be folded

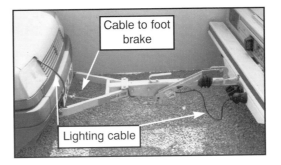

Cable to foot brake

Lighting cable

for storage in the boot of the car.) At the other end of the frame is a totally conventional caravan towing coupling for attachment to a standard tow ball. All this forms the RV and the car into a rigid structure. If the steering lock is now placed in the unlocked position, the car will follow the RV; when turning the front wheels of the car will castor. This is because the point of contact of the tyres with the ground is not vertically below the centre of their suspension but slightly to the rear; this is part of car design to introduce a tendency for the wheels to travel in a straight line, of their own accord.

What about the 750kg/four wheel braking rule? A cable links the foot brake and the coupling and is so arranged that when the coupling is compressed, ie when the RV is braked, the cable is pulled and the car brakes applied. The efficiency of this is improved if the tow ball is at such a height that the 'A' or 'Y' frame is riding slightly nose high. You might consider avoiding this braking difficulty by having a car weighing less than 750kg. A few do exist but the advice is that it is a good idea to have even these very light cars braked. Having said that, there is no USA requirement for any trailed car braking. Whether the car is below or above 750kg could be of some significance when 'new' drivers and those of RVs weighing more than 7.5 tonnes are considering their licence requirements.

When towing, you bring in another, clearly stated, limitation on your RV - the gross combined weight rating ie the maximum weight of the motorhome and any pulled load. It is most unlikely that you will come anywhere near this limit. With dinghy towing, this also applies to the maximum down load permitted on the tow ball. Consult your handbook/documentation to determine these figures.

Another legal requirement is for correct lighting and this is accomplished by linking the car lights to the RV lights through a normal towing

With close inspection the caravan coupling can be identified, the cable to the foot brake and the lighting cable going under the bonnet.

For driving tests after 1 January 1997, a C1 test (required for 3.5 to 7.5 tonnes) does not involve towing but the licence entitles you tow up to 750kg. A C1+E test has to be taken, which does involve demonstrating trailer skills, for a licence to tow more than 750kg. Similarly, if the letter of the law is being followed and a driver of a vehicle in excess of 7.5 tonnes takes his required C test, the licence covers a trailer up to 750kg. A C+E test is required for more than 750kg.

Details of
Car-a-Tow
are given in the
Appendix.

A DIY board for the back window of the car. Note the triangles.

'UK legal state'.
You might think
that this rule is
working against
you when it
comes to road
fund licence,
MoT etc. Even
if you are on a
long stay
abroad, it is a
requirement
that your
vehicle meets
UK legal
demands
eg current road
fund licence,
valid MoT and,
of course,
insurance.

lighting socket and a specially installed socket in the car's engine compartment. If all this sounds incredibly complicated, engineering-wise, then the good news is that there is a firm called Car-a-Tow which specialises in this modification and they make a very professional job of it.

The legality

With the modifications set out above, the car is considered to have become a trailer and the alterations mean that it conforms to trailer law - or so the installers and users of the system believe. Over the years, as this trailer law has become formulated, recreational towing of a car has not been a factor. So the rules do not take this into account but it does seem that it is accepted in this country as there have been no legal challenges. This is not the case abroad. To appreciate this, it is worth musing on how incredibly lax are our towing rules. With your car, you could tow a compatriot's vehicle, on a rope, from John O'Groats to Lands End and be legal. This is certainly not the case in Spain. The only such towing allowed is to remove a broken down or accident involved car that is causing an obstruction - and then only far enough to clear the traffic flow. Further movement must be done by a properly equipped towing vehicle. The French, though not quite as strict, lean towards this view. It has to be said, though, that many people have car-towed on the Continent without challenge. One also has to admit that the 'car on a trailer' fraternity do not have a problem.

In defence of Continental dinghy towing, there is an European Community argument that can be used, based on the rule that you, as a visitor to an EC country, can drive your vehicle legally even though it does not meet some aspect of the host country's legislation, providing the car is in a 'UK legal state'. A rather simplistic example of this is the colour of number plates. So, you might be able to argue that, as car towing is legal (well, allowed) here, then you should be OK abroad. Car-a-Tow's Alan Bee has produced some multi-lingual leaflets setting out this argument for the benefit of doubtful police officers. This brings up a practical point; such challenges are clearly the act of individual officers with an opinion. If that goes against you, at the roadside, then you politely accept the verdict, unhitch and drive off, separately. When you consider the coast to be clear, you re-hitch! Last Continental towing point: you will need to ascertain the attitude, towards a towed car, of

your chosen ferry company with regard to cost.

Further UK legalities

When towing, the car number plate should be obscured and that of the RV displayed. Car-a-Tow do a neat spring loaded, clip on number plate, which accomplishes this. Your combined outfit is long, so do you need to display a 'Long Vehicle' sign? My interpretation of The Highway Code (although it does use the term 'commercial vehicle') is that the answer is 'Yes' if the combined length is 13 metres or more (41ft 9ins) and is optional for 11 metres (35ft 4ins) to that 13 metres. Further interpretation of The Highway Code implies that the familiar triangular reflectors to indicate a towed load are optional - the reflectors on the car would do. You might think it a good idea to display triangles anyway so that everything, warning wise, is on your side. This applies to an 'On Tow' notice. I have combined the two; in the rear window of the car I have a board with the triangles and 'On Tow'. Additionally I have thought it a good idea to have a plate saying 'Towing' displayed on the front of the vehicle. In a confrontational situation on a narrow road, pointing to the sign does persuade the 'opposition' that the easiest solution is for them to back up!

Towing points

You will find that the car follows the RV incredibly well in normal driving situations. The only time you will see it is on roundabout, T-junction and the like turns. These need to be taken in such a way as to allow for the extra length and the fact the car will cut the corner, to some degree. There might be some doubt about how well the car follows with low speed, sharp turns; my experience is that, without momentum, the front car wheels do not castor readily and there is a tendency for the tyres to scrub. This sort of manoeuvring is likely to occur at the beginning and end of your journey, eg site departure and arrival, and so the simple solution is to have the car unhitched for these stages. We make use of this for our last two miles home. It is narrow, so we unhitch and my wife drives ahead, with dipped headlamps and hazard lights flashing (technically, for a car on the move, nonsensically illegal!) to warn oncoming traffic that our precious big vehicle is on its way.

With the car out of sight, most of the time, a risk has to be accepted with regard to car punctures. It is unlikely that you would realise something

The clue to the composition of this 'curtain' is the manufacturer - a brush company. It is made of long plastic bristles. I was disappointed with its efficiency and decided not to fit it to my new Winnebago. It was then I realised that it was cutting out a lot of the spray - not all, but every little helps!

A piece of wood that sits behind the tow ball will give protection in case of an over-run. If a vertical line is painted on this, lined up with the tow ball, it will help the aim of the driver.

was wrong in time to prevent wheel damage. One has to rely on the fact that the odds of a puncture are, hopefully, small.

One final 'downer' is that it is impossible to reverse your RV with the car attached; try to do so and you run a very high risk of damaging the attachment bracket and/or the associated parts of the car. This rather concentrates one's mind on navigation! We have only been in this 'having to reverse' situation a couple of times and the only answer is to unhitch and reposition. The inconvenience of this is greatly reduced if you can find a way of supporting the towing frame, with a cable, for the brief bit of car manoeuvring that you have to do.

Checks

It is vital that you are methodical about the hitching up process and that you then double check what you have done. With the car and RV united, check the ball coupling and frame lug attachments for security, that the safety break-away cable is clipped on and the foot brake cable is attached. Finally, on the outside, see that the coupling hand brake is off. Inside the car check the other end of the brake cable is attached to the foot brake, the car is out of gear and the hand brake is off. Finally, unlock the steering by turning the ignition key to the point where the warning lights are illuminated and then going back one click. If there are things

that run in this position eg the fan, the radio, then they obviously should be off. Physically check the steering wheel is free by a swing, left and right, of the steering wheel past the straight ahead position. If the initial drive off is going to be straight ahead then leave the steering wheel central. If an immediate turn of the RV is going to be required then bias the car's wheels in that direction. Finally, as a security precaution, lock all doors.

Some final points

You well know the filthy state your everyday car can get into if you drive close behind a lorry on a mucky day. On such a day, your poor towed car is going to complete a whole journey like that, so be prepared for some cleaning on arrival. The American RV market has solutions for everything; how efficacious they are can often be questioned. They offer two remedies for the 'dirty towed car syndrome'. One is a curtain along the rear of the RV; this can be solid plastic/rubber or made up of long bristles. I fitted one of the latter and found it only helps to some extent as an awful lot of the dirty spray spills around the sides of the motorhome. The second solution, perhaps one with more potential, is not really available to the UK market. This is a 'car bra' (!). Tailor-made for various makes of car, it is a cover for the front end.

Think about insurance. In the event of a claim,

There is a device called a Tyron Band which guards against a punctured tyre coming off and/or breaking up. It fits into the well of the wheel rim. Tyron Bands are fitted at TyreServices centres and the cost for four wheels is something less than £200.

Something you have to live with: when towing the mileage is recorded on the car's mileometer

would either your RV insurer or the one for your car, or both, be surprised that you were engaged in this strange exercise! It would perhaps be worth advising them of your intention.

Dinghy towing wins!

In spite of some early reservations about losing the great asset of a motorcaravan - that is its uncomplicated manoeuvrability, I now seldom travel without the car. It is a tremendous asset which changes one's motorhoming philosophy. We now tend to spend a lot more time in one location, content in the knowledge that we can get out and about over a large part of the local area. There have also been a tremendous number of combined business and pleasure, visiting relations and the like, trips that have only been possible with the car - and, in my opinion, the only way to tow that car is on its own four wheels!

A trip around the Isle of Mull, from The Caravan Club Site at Onich, would not have been possible without the towed car!

Having said that most USA towed cars are not braked, notice, on the weight sheet on page 54, that if a 'trailer' is unbraked then this affects the Gross Combination Weight Rating.

An American motorhome at the upper end of the RV size scale. It is a Winnebago Vectra on a Freightliner chassis. Note the slide-out. A vehicle of this specifications has a maximum weight in excess of 7.5 tonnes (16,500lbs). The owner is a believer in 'car in a trailer' towing. He has a unique way of overcoming the trailer handling difficulty and uses one of those 'electric movers' intended for caravan manoeuvring.

Car towing seems to lend itself to anecdotes:

'Où est votre billet, Madame?'
On the topic of towing, a magazine correspondent told the tale that he was stopped by the French toll motorway police and the only way he was allowed to proceed was to unhitch his car and his wife to drive it. The subsequent scene at the exit toll booth was not described!

An RV tower on a motorway was overtaken by a car that, a mile or so later, turned into a service area. The RV was stopping too. The car driver approached the RV owner who anticipated some of the usual questions. He was a bit astonished with this one: 'Do you have to tow the car with the engine running?' 'No, of course not,' retorted the RV man. 'Well,' replied the car driver, 'As I passed you just now it certainly sounded like it.' The RV owner thinks - and checks. He found that the car was in 2nd gear! Surprisingly there was no damage!

In the USA I saw a towed car with this notice in the rear:

I am sorry that I am driving slowly but I am having hell of job pushing this huge RV!

Hitching up is a two person job and can be a test of matrimonial harmony! Perhaps that is why the Americans have developed a tow bar that isn't rigid until you start the tow. During the hitching-up phase it can be moved from side to side and, to a limited extent, forward and back.

Security

It is a brave RV owner who does not take some extra precautions to protect his considerable investment. Some aspects of RV security are considered.

A rather naive person criticised 'The Motorcaravan Handbook' for painting too black a picture of the security aspects of motorcaravanning. The critic was obviously not a close follower of motorcaravan matters; each motorcaravan magazine usually seeks help by giving information on a theft - sometimes carried out quite audaciously. One coachbuilt was stolen from a supermarket car park whilst the owners were shopping; the vehicle was recovered but with the coachbuilt living element stripped off! Most thefts are from owners' driveways. So, whilst one does not wish to spread doom and gloom, it would be totally irresponsible not to consider security in a book of this nature.

The threat

At the risk of being an originator of some famous last words, I think that size is on the side of the RV when it comes to vehicle theft. An American motorhome is a bit of a conspicuous object and one would hope that this might deter the 'entrepreneur' who wants to 'move it on'. Perhaps the greater threat is from a break-in for the theft of contents, someone who wants a bit of a joy ride with a difference or from mindless vandalism. Whatever you yourself consider the threat, you undoubtedly will be looking for good door and locker locks. Fortunately, you get such quality with the American product. Many European motorcaravans are sadly lacking in the strength of door locks - and the door frames themselves. Backing up the physical aspect you need an alarm system which: protects those doors and lockers, gives a warning if glass is being broken, recognises movement inside the motorhome. Additionally, it should detect that the engine component is being interfered with and prevent unauthorised starting. It can be seen that you are looking for a setup that combines normal vehicle protection and the type of detection one associates with a house system.

Strikeback

There are a number of products on the market which claim to provide motorcaravan security. These are generally piecemeal elements such as movement detectors attached to the dashboard, external steering wheel locks and the like. You might not think that such devices match up to the sophistication - or value - of your RV. What is wanted is an integrated system designed specifically for the job of protecting an RV. There is one firm that specialises in this and that is Van Bitz of Taunton, run by Eddie Jones. I have used his services for three vehicles which is testament to the quality of his product and workmanship.

The components

All wiring is black, only Van Bitz holds the key to which wire is which; this provides a challenge to the skilful thief. Engine-wise, when the system is armed the engine cannot be started. Any attempt to immobilise the system by removing the vehicle battery will set off the siren. Vertically hinged doors eg the domestic door and the driver's door, have magnetic contact switches; doors with a horizontal hinge eg lockers, have tilt sensitive switches. Operation of any of these will set off the alarm. An external socket can be provided, at the rear of the motorhome, with a plug to which is wired a loop. This cable can be put through bicycles, round a trailer hitch etc. If it is disconnected or cut, the siren will be triggered. Inside the motorhome there are two detectors which 'look' down the interior to detect the movement of a person. There is also a microphone sensitive to glass being impacted.

There are a number of refinements: the alarm can be activated in a 'panic' situation. If you want to set the alarm whilst you are inside then this can be done by disabling the movement detector. This is also handy for pet owners who want to go out and leave their animals behind.

> When you are on the road, lock your locker doors and the domestic one. It would be all too easy for them to be interfered with whilst you are stopped at traffic lights or whatever.

There is a warning when the battery in the push button activator is getting low. There is an 'arming with sound' button and one for a silent mode. As deterrence is one of the aims of an alarm system then the bright flashing red light at the front windscreen is a vital component. This will flash in a particular way if the alarm has been activated during your absence. Multi-lingual warning notices are provided for the windows.

It can be seen that Eddie Jones has developed a comprehensive, integrated, tailor-made system to protect an RV.

Extra immobiliser

As you read on you might form the opinion that I am somewhat paranoid about security but each to his own; you can judge how far you want to go. One of my 'belt and braces' was to have an extra engine immobiliser fitted by Van Bitz. This is a highly sophisticated model that is automatically armed when the ignition is turned off. Thus, I have the satisfaction of knowing that there is always an element of protection and it is also there as another barrier to the thief.

More

Physical barriers can be another delaying factor. It has already been said that most thefts are from driveways. There are, on the market, a number of security posts. These are slotted into a receiver, concreted into the drive, and locked. Depending on your parking situation, it can be located to front or rear of the vehicle. Security lights for your drive are another thought.

One more thing

My final line of defence is very simple - a baby alarm! I put the transmitter on the RV coaming and the receiver is by my, rather distant, bed. If the alarm should go off - or there is undetected activity - then I will hear it.

Look around

Check over your RV to see if there are any weak points in its security. I locked myself out in my early days and it took the RAC man just two minutes to break in. He was able to release a sliding window catch. So that this could not be repeated, I made-to-measure strips of wood, painted black, to fit in the window channels.

Other security thoughts

After I locked myself out, I decided to go for two lines of defence against it happening again. Firstly, I made a wooden device to place in the slam door catch to prevent it being accidentally operated. It becomes a matter of habit to unlock the door and put it in place. Secondly, I have gone for the 'hidden key'. There are, literally, a thousand or more, accessible from the outside, places that you can hide a door key. I have done just that - more information is secret. As are details of another security device. I have adapted a piece of interior equipment, from its intended use, to act as a small 'safe'.

Better safe than sorry

I think it would be a very bold RV owner who does not take some extra steps to ensure that his expensive 'pride and joy' remains unviolated. We go on to consider some miscellaneous points of RV ownership.

I have caused some amusement amongst my friends when they hear about 'my baby' alarm - but it works!

This shaped piece of wood, hanging on a retaining chain, fits into the slot of the slam door lock lever.

Bits and pieces

T his chapter is devoted to a number of miscellaneous topics which arise from RV ownership. Most RVers take pride in their vehicles and this can lead to numerous essential and pleasurable activities.

This type of convector heater is very useful in a motorhome. During winter storage time it can be left switched on with the thermostat at on the 'Froststat' setting. During winter occupation, on a normal setting, it provides an ideal night-time background heat.

It might seem obtuse but one of the best ways of keeping your motorhome up together in the winter months is to use it! With the insulation and the facilities you have, it is very comfortable, even in the coldest weather.

Winterisation

Falling well and truly into the 'essential' bracket is care of your RV over the winter months. The vital thing here is to prevent damage through freezing of the water system. When the motorhome is not in use, the water should be drained. Your handbook will indicate where the drain valves are located. This will drain the fresh water tank but water could remain trapped in the pipes. A lot of this can be drained if, whilst you are emptying the fresh water tank, you open all the taps and hold the toilet open to the flush position with a piece of wood in the pedal mechanism. There should also be some valves that can be opened to assist this drainage - consult your handbook for location. All this is done, of course, with the water pump off. The hot water heater must also be drained and there will be a drain plug to accomplish this. With this draining routine, the enemy is air locks that can hold water in parts of the pipe system. I think it can help to drive with everything set in the draining condition, as outlined above. As winter approaches, or I have been on a winter trip, on my way home I stop and open all the appropriate valves and taps.

Further steps

You will find that your handbook goes into winterisation in some depth; the manufacturers have in mind the prolonged deep frosts that can be experienced in the USA. So you will read a suggestion of applying air pressure (not excessive) to the city water inlet to blow water out of the system. They might suggest that you disconnect the pipes to the water pump to ensure that it is

I think all RV owners long to have permanent under cover storage but that is denied to most of us. Here is a 'second best' idea - an RV cover. You will have to put it on your shopping list when you are on a visit to the States as they are not readily available in this country. I find it fantastic. With the motorhome washed, on goes the cover and it stays clean for the next trip - no black streaks! It is also cutting out UV damage, algae growth and many of the other evils that can attack your pride and joy!

fully drained. You perhaps will see reference to a water heater by-pass system. It is used in conjunction with potable anti-freeze. This is a special concoction that is readily available in the USA. Instead of draining the system you fill the pipes with this anti-freeze. The water heater, in the system, would take a lot of the liquid so this is by-passed and drained in the normal way. The word 'potable' is used above in the sense that when the system is flushed and brought back into use then the minute quantities of anti-freeze left will be harmless. It should go without saying that you should never use normal anti-freeze for this purpose.

My feeling is that we should match our precautions with the threat. We do get prolonged (week+) frosts but not very often. There is ample warning that this situation is developing and it is then that the more extreme measures can be adopted. For my part I feel I am keeping the threat at bay by background heating my RV. For non-critical times I use a low wattage heater that is fitted with a froststat. If it seems that the situation is going to become critical then more heaters can be utilised. The higher electricity bill is a small price to pay for the protection of an expensive vehicle. There is always the RV's blown air heating system to fall back on. Leave

below sink etc cupboard doors open - and the toilet compartment door - to allow the heat to spread to critical areas.

Flies

As with any activity, one lives and learns. With one of our motorhomes we learnt where flies go in the winter-time - one of the places is motor-

The USA cover featured is of a special soft material which breathes so problems of condensation and heat build up are eliminated.

My cleaning tools - a long handled Hozelock car washing brush and kitchen floor cleaner with a sponge head. No.2 Winnebago has a smooth roof so I have added a kitchen mop to my kit.

caravans! All those vents etc make a lovely winter home. Use your motorhome during those months and you find that you are providing a false summer and will have company. Now I use cut pieces of sponge rubber to fill all these openings, when the motorhome is not in use.

Further winter care

It goes without saying that, having spent a lot of money, care of your RV is a year-round job. Because perhaps you are not using it so much, if at all, then this should not mean that care should be suspended. Regular cleaning is still essential otherwise you will end up with a black streaked

monstrosity. Drawing the curtains and lowering the blinds is a good idea for any storage; this prevents the furnishings fading. Mechanically, you will need to consider your batteries and keep them charged. Engine-wise, there is a recommendation that you run the engine now and then until it reaches operating temperature. I think that there is a better answer - use your RV all year round. With all its facilities, it is comfortable even in the most hostile weather. A number of The Caravan Club Sites stay open all year, others into January.; opening time for most is late March.

Cleaning

Keeping an American motorhome clean might seem a daunting task but, firstly, you have your enthusiasm to lighten it. It might seem huge compared with a car but much of the bulk is big flat surfaces. The way to make the job easier is to have the right tools. I find a kitchen floor

cleaning tool with a sponge head incredibly useful. The long handle eliminates constant positioning and climbing up and down a step ladder. Having washed a side with a suitable detergent in warm water, a second useful tool comes into use; this is a long-handled car brush (Hozelock do a very good one). Again, the need for a ladder is eliminated. To finish the job, a chamois leather can be wrapped around the sponge head of the 'mop'. I find RV cleaning very satisfying - and after it, car washing tedious!

Caravans and motorcaravans suffer a common problem of black streaks down the sides. Many people believe that this is from rubber window surrounds etc but if you study these streaks you will see that this is not the reason; they can occur where there is no rubber. The cause is dirty rain and this shows up because the water constantly drains down the same lines due to construction features and the angle at which the outfit is parked - however slight. It is a good idea to tackle these marks, before starting the wash, with a non-scratching bathroom cleaner (Jif?). The reason for this initial assault is that, if you wet the surface, the marks will disappear only to reappear when dry.

Inner cleanliness

You are obviously going to tackle the inside of the RV in the same way as any household cleaning. When you are on your travels, a small handheld vacuum cleaner is useful. At home there is nothing like using the one from indoors. It pays to clean inside immediately after a trip to ensure that an interior staleness does not build up.

Summer protection

Summer deterioration is less obvious than winter but when we get one of those long hot spells then the temperature inside an RV can be incredibly high. With the blessing of all round insect proofing then it is a good idea to let the fresh air in through open doors and windows. For this situation, and for many others, I find Max-Air roof vent covers a real bonus. The motorhome can be ventilated without the fear of unexpected rain wetting the inside. It might seem that they cut down on the amount of air that can enter but I do not find this critical.

The Americans, with their very long, hot summers concern themselves about the effect of UV light on tyres. Covers can be purchased. You might consider this precaution worthwhile.

DIY

I find that a good deal of the pleasure that I derive from my motorhome is doing minor jobs and repairs that enhance its use.

A major task with a new RV is installing mains lighting which I find vastly superior to the 12volt sort - and it's cheaper on the bulbs! It should be emphasised that, unless you are a competent electrician, you should not contemplate interfering with the electrical system. But I have found it a simple job to fit extra, more convenient power points (not all to be used at once!) and mains lighting. The former can be spurs from the existing points. Mains lighting can be a wall lamp, downlights below cupboards and a bathroom mirror light. Simple and attractive mains lighting can be a table lamp and clip on spot lights. When doing these modifications I am very fussy about securing and hiding the wiring in a professional way.

The list of other jobs can be endless: wooden airing rails in the shower, display storage for a bedside clock, key rack, extra cupboard shelves, particularly for crockery, cutlery drawer divisions, lining cupboards and drawers with sound deadening, non-slip material - only your imagination is the limit on what can be done.

Handbook

With your motorhome there will be a substantial loose-leaf manual. One part will be a 'book'

The Max-Air roof vent covers can be seen in this photograph.

written by the converter; a substantial portion of the folder will be leaflets etc from the manufacturers of the various appliances and fittings. It pays to sift through this as you will find much extraneous material eg fitting instructions which might be useful for occasional reference but could be filed elsewhere. With some slimming down the folder will become more manageable. It pays then to start off a folder of your own for all the extra bits that you add eg electric kettle, fan heater and so on. A natural feature is a section for the vehicle registration document, insurance certificate and the like.

With the end of this book in sight, thoughts turn away from the UK scene to across the Atlantic. Before moving on to that topic, here are a few photographs of various RV 'bits and pieces'.

It is useful to build up a selection of electrical connectors:

1. A 'Continental' adaptor.

2. An adaptor allowing you to use a 15amp, 3-pin socket supply.

3. This lets you use your cable to supply a 3-pin socket.

4. A 'polarity reverser'. It is deliberately wired up with the live from the plug going to the neutral of the socket. Similarly, neutral goes to live. This enables you to correct 'reversed polarity' which is common on the Continent. See 'The Motorcaravan Handbook for more details.

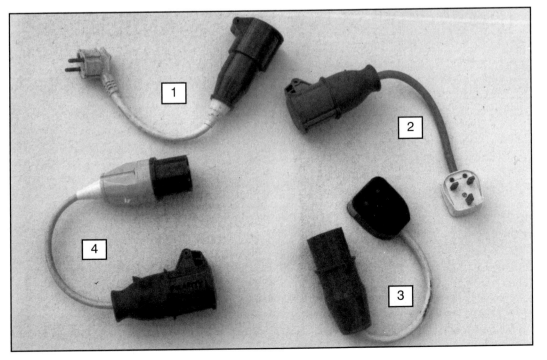

A DIY need! Motorcaravans seem to have a common failing of not having a rubbish bin. A normal size one is too big and if a smaller one can be found, it will be in the way. Ingenuity is called for:

1. Take a normal size lift-up lid type and mark a line all the way round it at a suitable height.

2. Cut to that line and make a bottom, cut to size, from MDF.

3. The finished product *in situ*.

4. It might be that a wall hanging bin would be more convenient. In this case cut a suitable original in half, vertically, in such a way as to preserve the lid hinge. A false back, with screw holes, is cut and fitted.

5. ... again - the finished product. These mini-bins are just the right size to take a plastic carrier bag.

1

2

1. A gimmick - but it can be interesting - an altimeter on the dashboard.

2. As with electrical connectors, you will build up a range of water ones. This is the most useful sort, which comes in three sizes, and will accommodate almost every shape and size tap that campsites can throw at you!

3

3. Returning to the awning topic, attention was drawn to the fact that it is a very large piece of vinyl to be flapping in a strong wind. Even a lighter wind can cause irritating movement and this can be substantially reduced with a pair of these restrainers. They do not obviate the need to retract the canopy if strong winds are expected. The rope is a, tailored to length, washing line which is very useful as it is shielded by the awning.

4

4. I count this as a classic DIY job. The need was somewhere suitable to stow the long sewer pipes; the location, all the spare space underneath the RV; the material, standard items from a builders' yard. The locker door, when closed, conceals the pipes from view.

The USA scene

Although this book is aimed at UK RV operating it does seem appropriate, and it might be useful for some, to consider the USA scene from two points: hiring and self importing - or a combination of both.

My experience

I have hired RVs on four occasions in North America and can recommend it as a superb way of seeing that continent. Our first hire was in Canada when we spent a fortnight in The Rockies - it was the best holiday I have ever had. Part of this might have been that it was our first experience of motorcaravanning. It certainly had its effect for we came home and bought our first outfit, a second-hand, but extremely little used, Bürstner low profile coachbuilt. Our

Our first motorhome a German Bürstner low profile coachbuilt.

trip to Canada was a short notice affair so we just went (to Edmonton) and checked into a hotel. We then studied the Yellow Pages, rang a hire company, took a taxi to examine what they had to offer and set off in a C-class the next day! On reflection, these number of years later, I think we were incredibly bold but the passing years and subsequent hires show that this first one was the most successful.

Our second hire, this time in the States, from a place I shall leave nameless, was a total disaster!

We used one of the UK companies that offers a complete package ie flight and vehicle hire. They are at the mercy of the operator of the franchise at your chosen pick-up location. In this case they were awful; we were totally let down with the dispatch to the extent that we had to make our first night stop a hotel. Then it became apparent that the vehicle was in a very poor state. When it started leaking like crazy, I'd had enough and protested on the headquarters hot line. This must have been fairly vociferous as I was offered the chance of returning the vehicle to the nearest franchise operator and a full refund. I think the fact that I said I was a travel writer helped! Incidentally, as I am going to recommend that you follow our Canadian example, you will need a back-up plan should you not be able to hire (highly unlikely). When we returned the second motorhome, we hired a car and continued on our tour with Bed & Breakfast. This is something that has grown in the States only in recent years and is conducted on a grander scale than over here. We found it a very pleasant and interesting way to travel.

Our third hire was OK - the motorhome was a little tired but it was cheap and was arranged by a relative resident in the USA. Our fourth 'hire' was a way not open to every one; we borrowed our, USA resident, youngest son's fifth wheel.

Campgrounds

RVs are big business in the States - there are millions and so the country is geared to them. Dealerships abound, accessory shops and bulk

gas supplies are plentiful, at every turn there seems to be a campground. It is worth purchasing a campground guide book - an excellent one is done by Woodalls. Every category of site is listed from the very elaborate commercial type to the humblest, no facilities, sort. The State Parks appealed to us; there are similar ones run by the Corps of Engineers as part of a reservoir, flood control scheme and the like and by the forestry organisation. All these are superbly set in carefully preserved natural surroundings. Some of the State Parks are unbelievably big. For all their naturalness, many of them have full hook-up (ie water, electricity and sewer) on each pitch. This is governed by State policy and does vary. Whether your choice is these or the very acceptable commercial sites, there are plenty.

Cost of living

If you are a motorcaravanner you will know how well you can control your expenditure - sometimes you can live for the same cost on the road as you do at home; or you can splash out a bit. Things are no different in the USA. The supermarkets are huge and the prices generally lower than ours. This is balanced out by the fact

A wealth of picnic tables at our West Virginia campground - which is probably an indication of the high occupancy in the busy season.

The campground notice to the left seems rather aggressive but it is the only real regimentation there is in the State Parks.

Our third RV hire outside our son's house in Pennsylvania.

This photograph demonstrates the scale of 'leisure' in the USA. It is part of The Blue Ridge Parkway which extends 469 miles along the crests of the Southern Appalachians and links two eastern national parks - Shenandoah and Great Smokey Mountains. It is a full two lane highway, with a 35mph speed limit. Commercial vehicles are barred as it is intended only for leisure motoring. This is the Linn Cove Viaduct which was constructed to make the final link in the road and had to skirt the rugged and rocky perimeter of Grandfather Mountain in North Carolina. We travelled, in an RV, the full length of this scenic highway.

that anything involving service is dearer - a haircut comes to mind! But eating out can be very good value. The majority of RVs are petrol-engined and you are looking at miles per gallon in the order of eight or nine - but fuel is nearly a third of our price. Hire charges equate very closely to the combined cost of car hire and motel accommodation. The figure is going to vary (increase?) with time and be subject to the rate of exchange and so I hesitate to give a positive price - but to give you a rough idea you

should be looking at something in excess of $100 per day.

Where and when to go
The choice is yours; with a country so vast, you have the full range of scenery and climate. There are two things I would warn about: many parts of the States have severe winters, short springs and autumns (falls) sandwiching very hot and humid summers. On our last trip we experienced the 90s - both in degrees Fahrenheit and percentage humidity. This severely limits what you can or feel like doing. An aspect of the vastness is that huge areas of the country have very similar scenery. In the UK it would be possible to be in the Highlands of Scotland one day and the flat of Norfolk the next. We spent three months travelling Virginia, Tennessee, North Carolina and West Virginia and we never really escaped from mountains and trees!

All in all, I can heartily recommend North America; not the least of the attraction being that you can enjoy the use of an RV in its natural environment.

Self importing
Go to the States and you will be drawn to the RV dealerships, just to have a look around.

Your appetite whetted, you will be interested in prices - but you will most likely find none. If there are any then they will be totally misleading. This is the strange American way with vehicles. You show an interest, the dealer gives you a price, you make a lower offer, he throws in some extras - and so it goes on. It is the sort of dealing I hate as I am no good at it! But, in spite of this state of affairs, you will get a feel for the prices and if you have studied the UK RV prices you will be astonished, if the exchange rate is favourable, at the value for money. It won't be long before you think, 'Why don't I go the USA with my cash, buy an RV, use it for an extended tour (six/nine months?) and then ship it back to the UK?'

You will not be the pioneer that you might think; this road has been trod by many before you. But if it is as attractive as it sounds why aren't the UK RV dealers queuing up at the Job Centre?

A personal view

You may not agree with any of the following which probably makes you a bolder person than I. My main objection to self importing is the enormous number of risk areas. This starts at the dealership where we have already seen that, particularly as one is not accustomed to American ways, you could easily be 'seen off'. One major disadvantage, with future UK operation in mind, is that you will, almost certainly, have to buy a petrol-engined model. Diesel, on the home market, is rare in the States where the price of petrol is not a factor. The vehicle is now yours and you set off on your travels. What happens if anything goes wrong, which it inevitably will with a vehicle of such complexity? You might persuade another dealer to fix it under the warranty - I have my doubts. Having had your holiday it is time for shipping. Say farewell to your 'pride and joy' at the dockside and hand over the keys - and start to pray. Prayers against dockside damage, theft and vandalism, against accelerated wear and tear brought on by deck cargo transportation, against dealing with a UK customs officer who has had a bad day. As you drive away from Southampton, or wherever, are your troubles at an end? Well, who is going to carry out the considerable number of modifications to make the RV legally and conveniently operable in the UK? Vehicle lighting and 240volt provision are major areas. One of the dealers will do this for you - at a price. He will also want his

due to fix any faults that you have - your warranty is dead. But, all this is my dismal view; ask someone who has done it and they might tell you a different story, coloured no doubt by the tendency in human nature to gloss over any past difficulties.

Some importation rules

If you do decide to go for self importing then you are going to get some idea of the import rules from HM Customs and Excise. There are a couple of surprises here. Firstly, there is a common belief that if you own a vehicle abroad for a period of time then you will be exempt duty etc. There is a degree of truth in this but the qualifying period is 12 months. So, unless you have a very long holiday you will be paying import duty. The value of your vehicle will be assessed, supported by your invoices, to this is added, believe it or not, the cost of shipping and insurance and 10% of this dockside total is the import duty. VAT at 17.5% is now levied on that dockside total plus the import duty.

Your eyes might be watering a bit by now. Your costs so far are: the original purchase price, the cost of shipping and insurance, the import duty and VAT. Now comes the previously mentioned essential modification work. The margin between the USA purchase price and UK one has been considerably narrowed.

America!

It is my experience that RV ownership makes you, or increases a tendency to be, pro-American. Try it!

Gold Motor Service Company, of Alton, specialise in RV modification and rectification work. This includes the conversion of automotive lighting and domestic mains wiring to UK standards.

Self importers need to keep in mind the width limits referred to on page 14.

A final shot to whet your appetite - Mabry Mill on The Blue Ridge Parkway.

Conclusion

This has been a long road through the land of UK RV ownership. On the journey I trust you have been buoyed along by my enthusiasm and inspired to try your own route.

At the start I did say that this is a very personal view of RVing but I hope that, even if it does not match your aspirations, you will find the information of some value in starting off. The contents should have persuaded you to buy wisely, operate safely and successfully and get the maximum pleasure from your own 'dream machine'. There is no vehicle quite like an American motorhome.

I hope that you are tempted to contact some or all of the various UK RV dealers to see what they have to offer.

I wish you happy RVing!

Appendices:

Glossary
Useful addresses
Index
Conversion tables

Glossary

Many UK motorcaravanning terms have been included to enable the reader to make comparisons between the USA and UK scene. A fuller explanation of many of the items is contained in the text; please see the index.

A-CLASS: A type of motorcaravan where the converter has only used the chassis, engine and driving controls of the base vehicle.

ALCOVE BED: A bed (usually double) built over the top of the cab of a coachbuilt. Also known as a luton bed.

AMPERAGE: The strength of current of electricity expressed in amperes (abbreviation amps). The amperage of an appliance is the strength of current that it will draw; the amperage of a supply is the strength of current it can supply.

AMPS: Abbreviation for amperes (see AMPERAGE).

AUTOMATIC TRANSMISSION: A mechanism which automatically changes gear, eliminating the clutch control.

BASE VEHICLE: The commercial vehicle on which a motorcaravan conversion is based.

BASE WEIGHT: One term for the weight of a motorcaravan as supplied by the converter ie none of the owner's items are on board. (US term: UNLOADED VEHICLE WEIGHT).

BASIC WEIGHT: Alternative for base weight.

BLACK WATER: US term for chemical toilet contents (see GREY WATER).

BUTANE: One type of liquid petroleum gas for motorcaravan use. It is supplied in blue containers and is not suitable for cold weather use. (See PROPANE).

C-CLASS: The American term for a coachbuilt

CALOR GAS: The major UK supplier of liquid petroleum gas.

CAMPING AND CARAVANNING CLUB, THE: One of the clubs in the UK for campers, caravanners and motorcaravanners.

CAMPING CARD INTERNATIONAL: A document (card) that is available to members of The Caravan Club, The Camping and Caravan Club and some other organisations which provides Third Party liability cover, when foreign touring, for members and those in their party. Valid for one year, it is accepted world-wide as an identity document and can be deposited with camping site administration instead of a passport.

CAMPING CARNET: The old, but still used, term for the Camping Card International.

CAMPING GAZ: A brand of butane aimed at the outdoor recreation market. Sizes of container vary from small disposable ones for hikers up to bigger refillable ones. Only the largest size of the latter (the 907) is likely to interest the motorcaravanner; even this is small compared with Calor Gas cylinders. The great advantage of Camping Gaz is that it is widely available on the Continent and elsewhere.

907 Camping Gaz cylinder ...

... compared with a 13kg Calor Gas one.

CAR DOLLY: A two wheel device on to which can be secured the front wheels of a car for towing. It is of interest to motorcaravanners for towing a small car behind their outfits but its legality for this purpose is debatable.

CARAVAN CLUB, THE: The premier UK club specialising in providing facilities for caravanners and motorcaravanners.

CARAVAN SITES AND CONTROL OF DEVELOPMENT ACT 1960: Legislation to

limit and control the development of caravan sites.

CARBON MONOXIDE (CO): A highly poisonous, inflammable, colourless, odourless gas formed by the incomplete combustion of carbon or carbon compounds. The classic source is car exhaust fumes.

An RV's ceiling mounted carbon monoxide detector - part of the standard fittings. For LPG detection, a floor mounted detector is required. The safety scene is completed with a smoke detector.

CASSETTE BLIND: A motorcaravan window device with a roller top and bottom giving three choices of window covering, a night blind, a fly screen or nothing at all.

CASSETTE TOILET: A form of chemical toilet with the facility of having the waste and chemical toilet fluid entirely isolated from the lavatory bowl and contained in a cassette (moulded plastic box). This can be taken separately to a disposal point for emptying.

CERTIFICATED LOCATIONS: A result of the Caravan Sites and Control of Development Act 1960 which allowed smaller sites to operate provided they were vetted by an approved organisation. The Caravan Club is such an

The access to a motorcaravan's cassette toilet.

The sign at the entrance to the new Caravan Club Site at Edinburgh.

organisation and 'certificated location' is their term for small sites licensed to have up to five members' outfits at a time subject to a maximum stay by any one member of 28 days. They are generally sites offering only limited facilities but are quiet and unspoilt.

CHASSIS-CAB: The elements of a base vehicle on which a coachbuilt is based.

CHASSIS-SCUTTLE: The elements of a base vehicle on which an A-class is based.

CHOPPED VAN: US term to describe various motorhomes: the converter has 'chopped' the 'van'. If this 'chopping' leaves the cab then a coachbuilt (qv) results. If the cab has been 'chopped' as well then the outcome is an A-class (qv). A 'chopped van - low profile' is, as its name implies, a coachbuilt with low height, typically less than eight feet.

This Winnebago Rialta is an example of a 'chopped van - low profile'.

Photo: Winnebago Industries

The RV's city water connection.

CITY WATER: American motorhomes generally have the facility to connect their water system direct to a site tap, assuming that there is exclusive use. The domestic water in the motorhome then works at mains pressure, bypassing the pump (and tank). The term for this is 'city water'.

CLUB SITES: The term used by The Caravan Club for their large, generally full facility, sites.

COACH: The American term for 'domestic' i.e. coach battery = domestic battery.

COACHBUILT: A motorcaravan where the converter has used the cab, engine and chassis of the base vehicle and 'coachbuilt' a living unit on the back.

COMMUNAL AERIAL: A facility provided at some sites where the TV reception is poor. A boosted signal from a sophisticated aerial is passed, via cable, to various points on the site. A fee is charged for the use of the plug-in points.

CONTROL PANEL: A facility for monitoring and operating the electrical, and possibly other, systems in a motorcaravan. It could have a mains master switch, domestic battery control switch, vehicle and domestic battery voltmeters, switches for lights, water pump, water heater and contents gauges for fresh and waste water tanks.

CONVERTER: A company that 'converts' base vehicles into motorcaravans.

CRUISE CONTROL: A device that allows the driver to set a particular cruising speed which will then be automatically controlled. It is possible to accelerate or decelerate without disengaging. On braking, cruise control is automatically cut out.

DECLARED MAXIMUM WEIGHT: The maximum weight to which the motorcaravan should be loaded. (US term: GROSS VEHICLE WEIGHT RATING).

DEEP CYCLE BATTERY: A battery that is used for the 'domestic' part of a motorcaravan with design features making it suitable for a continual 'cycle' involving discharge to a low level followed by a recharge. This is a requirement for a domestic battery as opposed to a vehicle battery where a big initial power surge is needed for engine starting and, hopefully, the battery is then not allowed to go flat.

DINGHY TOWING: An American expression for towing a car on its own four wheels.

DISMOUNTABLE: A form of motorcaravan where the living unit is mounted on the flat bed of a pick-up truck and can be removed and stored when not required. (US term: TRUCK CAMPER).

DOGBONE ADAPTOR: A US term for an adaptor to connect the plug of a motorhome hook-up cable to a domestic socket.

DOLLY: A two-wheeled device to take the front wheels of a car so that it can be towed.

DOMESTIC: The motorcaravan term applied to anything associated with the living aspect of the outfit as opposed to the vehicle side (ie domestic door).

DOMESTIC BATTERY/IES: Additional battery/ies provided in motorcaravans to power the 12 volt electrical facilities in the caravan portion of the vehicle.

DORMOBILE: Trade name for a motorcaravan of the 1950s/60s which is used, by some, as a name for motorcaravans in general.

DOUBLE POLE SWITCH: An electrical switch which, when in the OFF position, breaks both the live and neutral wiring. This type of switch is in common use on the Continent (see SINGLE POLE SWITCH and REVERSED POLARITY).

DUMP STATION: A sewage and waste water facility for motorcaravans, in particular American motorhomes, which need positioning by a disposal point for the discharge of their black and grey water tank contents through a flexible pipe directly into a sewer.

EARTH TRIP: An outdated device, but still used term, for detecting a fault in an electrical system and tripping the supply (see RESIDUAL CURRENT DEVICE).

FAUCET: US term for a water tap.

FIFTH WHEEL: A caravan designed to be towed by a pick-up truck. The forward portion is stepped up to fit over the bed of the truck on to which is mounted the coupling. The outfit is thus articulated.

FLY CAMPING: An alternative term for wild camping.

FURNACE: In motorhome parlance, the US term for the gas heating system.

GAS CONTAINERS: Liquified Petroleum Gas (LPG) is supplied in a variety of containers to suit different uses.

Canisters are small and disposable, designed to fit specific appliances (ie picnic stoves, lamps). They are aimed mostly at the backpacker.

Cylinders or Bottles are heavy metallic containers of varying sizes of a range to suit the smallest motorcaravan up to those intended for static domestic situations. The cylinders are rechargeable. In the UK this is normally done at a central plant and the consumer locally exchanges an empty cylinder for a full one. Some continental systems employ bulk dispensers and the consumer's cylinder is refilled on the spot. This is also a common way with this type of cylinder in the USA where they are known as DOT (Department of Transportation) cylinders. There are also cylinders which are exchanged ie in line with our system.

Tanks are, in the motorcaravan gas context, a permanently installed, frame mounted, below floor, gas storage facility requiring refilling

from a bulk dispenser. They are a common feature of American motorhomes but some UK firms do specialise in modifying European models. In the USA these are known as ASME (American Society of Mechanical Engineers) tanks.

GASLOW SAFETY GAUGE: A commercial device for indicating the contents of a gas cylinder. It can also give signs that there is a leak in the system.

GFCI: Abbreviation for ground fault circuit interrupter (qv).

GREEN CARD: In fact, a green paper form provided by vehicle insurance companies for overseas travel. Its issue indicates the degree to which the company has agreed to extend the insured cover for such travel and should always be obtained beforehand. There may be a charge for the additional cover.

GREY WATER: US term for the contents of a sink/shower/washbasin waste water tank (see BLACK WATER).

GROSS AXLE WEIGHT RATINGS: US term for the maximum weights that the front and rear axles should carry.

GROSS COMBINED WEIGHT: A term for gross train weight.

GROSS COMBINATION WEIGHT RATING: US term for the maximum allowable loaded weight of a motorhome with its towed trailer.

GROSS TRAIN WEIGHT: The UK term for the total permitted maximum weight of a motorcaravan and any pulled load.

GROSS VEHICLE WEIGHT RATING: The US term for the absolute maximum permissible weight that a particular motorhome should weigh. The gross vehicle weight rating is equal to or greater than the sum of the unloaded vehicle weight plus the net carrying capacity.

GROUND FAULT CIRCUIT INTERRUPTER: The US equivalent of our residual current device (qv). It is usually part of a 120 volt wall socket (receptacle) manifesting itself as a red button. If the protection is activated the button will pop out and isolate that socket and others on the same circuit.

HARDSTANDING: A pitch with a hard surface that can be used in all weathers.

HEIGHT BARRIER: A horizontal bar erected at the entrances to car parks etc. to limit the height of vehicles using the facility.

HIGH TOP: A term for the type of motorcaravan where the converter has used a panel van and provided permanent standing height room in the living area by removing the original roof and substituting a higher one.

HOLDING TANK: Permanently installed tank to hold black or grey water.

HOOK-UP: The facility at a pitch to provide a suitably equipped motorcaravan with mains electricity The term might also be applied to water, television and telephone supply and a sewer outlet.

HOT WIRE: US term for the electrical live wire.

INTEGRAL: A term sometimes used for an A-class.

INVERTER: 'Inverts' 12 volt DC to AC. This can be 120 volt or 240 volt, depending on model.

LAVATORY OR LAVATORY BASIN: The US term for a washbasin.

LIQUEFIED PETROLEUM GAS: Energy gas that has been pressurised to the point where it has changed to a liquid. It is kept under pressure, for subsequent use, in a gas container.

LPG: Abbreviation for liquefied petroleum gas.

LUTON: The term for a coachbuilt motorcaravan body shape which extends over the cab and usually provides space for a double bed.

MASS: The scientifically correct term for weight and one being increasingly used in defining weight limits.

MAXIMUM OVERALL WEIGHT: see GROSS MAXIMUM WEIGHT.

MUNICIPAL SITES: Sites in France provided by local authorities in conjunction with the French equivalent of British Chambers of Commerce.

NET CARRY CAPACITY: The US term for the maximum weight of all occupants, including the driver, personal belongings, food, fresh water, LP gas, tools, tongue weight of towed trailer, dealer installed accessories, that can be loaded by the owner.

NOSE WEIGHT: The downward force (weight) exerted on a tow ball by a tow bar. (US term: TONGUE WEIGHT).

OMNI-DIRECTIONAL TV AERIAL: A TV signal comes from a transmitter to a location in a specific direction. An omni-directional aerial will pick up that signal (with varying degrees of success) without the need for the aerial to be aimed at the transmitter (see YAGI AERIAL).

OUTFIT: General term to cover motorcaravan, caravan, trailer tent etc. (Alternative US term: RIG).

P AND T VALVE: Pressure and temperature relief valve (qv).

PANEL VAN: The name for a commercial light delivery van which generally has metal 'panel' sides. It is a popular type of base vehicle for UK motorcaravan converters.

PAS: Abbreviation for power assisted steering.

PAYLOAD: Another term for net carrying capacity.

PDI: Abbreviation for the pre-delivery inspection.

PITCH: The area on a site chosen or allocated for locating an outfit.

PITCH POST: The means of identifying a pitch.

PLATED AXLE WEIGHT: Another term for gross axle weight ratings.

POLARITY: In electrical terms, polarity refers to the positive (or live) and negative (neutral) flows of current. The associated wiring is coloured brown and blue, respectively. On a correctly wired UK supply, the current should flow from the supply through the positive wire then via a switch to the interior of the appliance and thence back to the source via the neutral (see REVERSED POLARITY).

POLARISATION: In TV terms, the signal has either horizontal or vertical polarisation and the elements of a yagi aerial have to be aligned on the appropriate plane to receive the signal.

POTABLE: A term indicating drinking water.

POWER CONVERTER: an RV transformer and rectifier ie it takes 120 volt AC and converts it to 12 volt DC. The unit also usually includes a battery charger and the motorhome 120 volt circuit breakers and 12 volt fuses.

PRE-DELIVERY INSPECTION: The inspection which should be carried out by the dealer prior to sale.

PRESSURE AND TEMPERATURE RELIEF VALVE: A valve fitted to the water heater, accessible through the outside hatch, which guards against excess pressures and temperatures in the heater. It is normal for it to drip hot water, now and then. It should be exercised (with the water pump/city water off) from time to time, taking care that the hot water that escapes does not scald.

PROPANE: One type of liquid petroleum gas for motorcaravan use. It is supplied in red containers and is suitable for cold weather use (see BUTANE).

RCCB: An abbreviation for Residual Current Circuit Breaker.

RCD: An abbreviation for Residual Current Device.

RECEPTACLES: The US term for electrical sockets.

The BIG Winnebago Brave - a 33RQ - DL. Note the slide-out.

RECREATIONAL VEHICLE: The US term for a motorcaravan, motorhome, fifth wheel etc.

REGULATOR: In motorcaravan gas supply terms, the device for controlling the pressure of the supply of gas from its container to the appliances. It is a part of the permanent installation in an RV gas system.

RESIDUAL CURRENT CIRCUIT BREAKER: This device was superseded by the Residual Current Device.

RESIDUAL CURRENT DEVICE: An electrical device for detecting a fault in an electrical system and instantaneously isolating the supply. (US term: GROUND FAULT CIRCUIT INTERRUPTER qv).

REVERSED POLARITY: In electrical terms, a situation where the polarity flow has been reversed ie the flow is entering the appliance via the neutral wire and leaving via the live. This situation would arise if the brown wire was attached to the neutral terminal of a 3-pin plug and the blue one to live. The appliance would still work but a potentially dangerous situation exists if the appliance has a single pole switch. It is a common feature on the Continent because they use double pole switches as opposed to our single poles ones. With the former, which wire is the live one is of no consequence.

RIG: American term for a motorcaravan, generally the larger motorhome or RV.

RISING ROOF: A type of motorcaravan where the converter has provided a portion of the roof that can be raised to give standing room inside.

RV: Abbreviation for recreational vehicle.

SHIPPING LENGTH: The absolute total length of a vehicle. A ferry company usually wants to know the shipping length of a motorcaravan at the time of booking.

SHORE LINE: An American expression, borrowed from the boating world, for the cable between the motorcaravan and the site's electrical supply.

SINGLE POLE SWITCH: An electrical switch which, when in the OFF position, only isolates the cable intended to carry the live supply (ie not the neutral). This is the common type of switch used on appliances in the UK (see DOUBLE POLE SWITCH).

Photo: Winnebago Industries

SITE: A facility providing pitches for caravans, motorcaravans, trailer tents and possibly tents.

SOCKET TESTER: An electrical device for checking for reversed polarity and other wiring faults. Note: such a tester should not be left permanently in a socket.

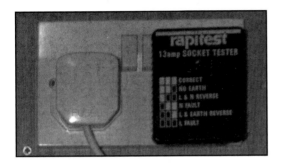

START WEIGHT or STARTING WEIGHT: see BASE WEIGHT.

SUPER PITCHES: The provision of pitches with multiple facilities ie water, electricity, TV, telephone, sewer outlet etc.

TARE WEIGHT: An older, and less precise term, for base weight.

THETFORD: The major manufacturer of chemical toilets.

THREE-WAY: A term applied to refrigerators that can be operated by mains electricity, gas or the vehicle battery (when the engine is running).

TONGUE WEIGHT: The US term for nose weight of trailer ie the downward force (weight) exerted on a tow ball by a tow bar.

TRAVEL TRAILER: US term: a conventional travel trailer is equivalent to a UK caravan - though some of them can be very large. A fifth wheel (qv) is also classed as a travel trailer. A park trailer is like UK 'statics'.

TRUCK CAMPER: US term for a dismountable (qv).

TYPE B: See VAN CAMPER.

TYPE C: US term for a coachbuilt (qv).

UNLADEN WEIGHT: Another term for base weight.

UNLOADED VEHICLE WEIGHT: The US term for a motorhome as built at the factory with full fuel, engine oil and coolants. The unloaded vehicle weight does not include cargo, fresh water, LP gas, occupants or dealer installed accessories.

VAN CAMPER: US term for a motorcaravan based on a panel van. Sometimes referred to as a Type B.

VEHICLE EXCISE DUTY: The correct term for the Road Fund Licence or Road Tax.

WHEELBASE: The distance between the points of ground contact of the front and rear wheels of a vehicle.

It is amazing what one accumulates in an RV! This photograph was taken on the occasion of the changeover to the new Brave.

Addresses and other information

This list has been compiled in an attempt to be helpful. It is simply a collection of firms and companies etc that have advertised in the motorcaravanning press. Inclusion in it is not an implied endorsement, neither should it be deduced that those not mentioned are not to be recommended.

Dealers, importers etc

Born Free (Europe)

Marneweg 19, 8701 PM, Bolsward, Netherlands
Tel: (31) 515 575800
Custom-made Born Free coachbuilts.

Brownhills

A1/A46 Junction, Newark, Notts NG24 2EA
Tel: 01636 704201
Fleetwood

Classic Camping

54 Hazelbank Road, Chertsey, Surrey KT16 8PB
Tel: 01932 568402
Great West Van

Dudleys American Motorhomes

A415 Abingdon Road, Ducklington, Witney, Oxon OX8 7XA
Tel: 01993 703774/774040
Coachman, Safari, Trail Wagon, Winnebago

Freedom Motorhomes

Mill Avon Holiday Park, Gloucester Road,
Tewkesbury, Glos GL20 5SW
Tel: 01684 293999
Pre-owned and commission sales

Gold Motor Sales

Unit 1 Caker Stream Road, Mill Lane Industrial Estate,
Alton, Hants GU34 2QA
Tel: 01420 544482
Scotty

Midland International RV Center

Wall Hill Road, Allesley, Coventry CV5 9EL
Tel: 01203 336411
Four Winds, Georgie Boy

Niche Marketing

Park House, Park Lane, Manby, Lincs LN11 8UF
Tel: 01507 327172
Adventure RV Mfg dismountables and fifth wheels

The Outback Import/Export Company

1 The Outback, Middle View Mobile Home Park, Normandy,
Guildford, Surrey GU3 2AZ
Tel: 01483 236567
Fifth Wheels

Southern Cross Motorhome Centre	Pantiles Park, London Road (A30), Bagshot, Surrey GU19 5HN Tel: 01276 452111
Travelworld American Motorhomes	Stafford Road, Wolverhampton, WV10 6HL Tel: 01902 420724 *Gulf Stream Coach, Monaco*
Wellsbridge Sales	Ramsey Forty Foot, Ramsey, Huntingdon, Cambs PE171XJ Tel: 01487 812901/815511 *Secondhand sales*
Westcroft American Motorhomes	Cannock Road, Westcroft, Wolverhampton WV10 8QU Tel: 01902 731324 *Allegro, Damon, Coachmen*
West Midland American Vehicles Ltd	Watling Street, Wedges Mills, Cannock, Staffs WS11 1TE Tel: 01543 462891

Servicing

Most of the dealers listed above carry out servicing. The following firms advertise as specialists:

American Parts	Tel: 01205 480077
Frenchie's American Service Centre	Woodville, Wisbech Road (A141), Westry, March, Cambs PE15 0BA Tel: 01354 658318
Gold Motor Service Co.	Unit 1 Caker Stream Road, Mill Lane Industrial Estate, Alton, Hants GU34 2QA Tel: 01420 544482
Rodley Motors	26 East Parade, Bradford BD1 5HD Tel: 01274 729425
Transatlantic Auto Services	Steve Marshall Tel: 01246 862813
West Midland American Vehicles Ltd	Watling Street, Wedges Mills, Cannock, Staffs WS11 1TE Tel: 01543 462891

Satellite TV

Aerial Techniques	11 Kent Road, Parkstone, Poole, Dorset BH12 2EH Tel: 01202 738232
Clearview	173 Kings Road, Kingston-upon-Thames, Surrey Tel: 0181 974 9098
Taskmaster Leisure	E8 Leodis Court, Leeds LS11 5JJ Tel: 0113 246 9555
Teleco	46 Main Road, Biggin Hill, Kent TN16 3DU Tel: 01959 574707/574969

Security

Van Bitz   Cornish Farm, Shoreditch, Taunton, Somerset TA3 7BS
                                Tel: 01823 321992

Insurance

Adrian Flux Insurance   Tel: 01553 777888

**Basildon Insurances   The Property Centre, Southernhay, Basildon, Essex SS14 1EB
Services Ltd**   Tel: 01268 527722

Comfort Insurance   391 Green Street, Upton Park, London E13 9AU
                                Tel: 0181 470 1127

Drewe Insurance   The Old Post House, 14 Load Street,
                                Bewdley, Worcs DY12 2AE
                                Tel: 01299 401663

Gibson Insurance   170 Green Street, Enfield EN3 7BR
                                Tel: 0990 134772

Jardine Faber   Saxon House, 39 Marefair, Northants NN1 1BR
                                Tel: 01604 639011

Motor Caravan Insurance Ltd 34 New Street, St Neots, Cambs PE19 1NQ
                                Tel: 01480 218273

Motorhome Ticket Club   2 Gillard Road, Brixham, Devon TQ5 9EG
                                Tel: 01803 855555

Safeguard   Charles House, Low Lane, Horsforth, Leeds LS18 5JA
                                Tel: 0113 258 1614

**Whittlesey Insurance   12 Queen Street, Whittlesey, Peterborough PE7 1AY
Services Ltd**   Tel: 01733 208117

Magazines

**Motorcaravan Motorhome   The Maltings, Manor Lane, Bourne, Lincs PE10 9PH
Monthly (MMM)**   Tel: (Subscriptions) 01778 391134

**Motor Caravan   Subscriptions Department, Bradley Pavilions,
Magazine (MCM)**   Bradley Stoke North, Bristol BS12 0BQ
                                Tel: 01454 620070

American RV Magazine   AB Publishing, (ARVM), Freepost (LE4684)
                                Leicester LE4 9BR
                                Tel: 0116 276 9921

Motorhome Monthly   Tel: 0181 302 6069

The Caravan Club Magazine is free to members.

Car towing

Car-a-Tow Ltd Unit 1, 565 Blandford Road, Hamworthy,
Poole, Dorset BH16 5BW
Tel: 01202 632488

Clubs

The Caravan Club East Grinstead House, East Grinstead, West Sussex RH19 1UA
Freephone for membership enquiries: 0800 521161

**The Camping
& Caravanning Club** Greenfields House, Westwood Way, Coventry CV4 8JH
Tel: 01203 694995

American RV Club Membership enquiries, Gina Brown, 50 Holford Road,
Durleigh, Bridgewater, Somerset TA6 7NT
Tel: 01278 446796

**American Motorhome Club
UK No. 1** Membership secretary, Les Slipper, GB Engineering, Unit 2,
Eagle House, Essex Road, Hoddesdon, Herts

**ARVE
(American RV Enthusiasts)** Paul Rees, 33 Cannock Street, Leicester LE4 9HR
Tel: 0116 276 9921

RV products

Camco Products Division Alde International (UK) Ltd, Sandfield Close,
Moulton Park, Northampton NN3 6AB
Tel: 01604 494193

American Parts Tel: 01205 480077

Miscellaneous

BBC Engineering Information White City, 201 Wood Lane, London W12 7TS
Tel: 0181 752 5040

Thetford Ltd Centrovell Industrial Estate, Caldwell Road,
Nuneaton, Warwickshire CV11 4UD
Tel: 01203 341941

UK Motorhome Hire Midland International RV Center, Wall Hill Road,
Allesley, Coventry CV5 9EL
Tel: 01203 336411

If you require further copies of this book then they can be obtained from:

Keyham Books, Startley, Chippenham SN15 5HG

Please make cheques for £12.99, which includes p&p, payable to David Berry.

Index

Conversion tables

To convert:	Into:	Multiply by:
Consumption		
Litres per kilometre	Imperial gallons per mile	0.354006
Imperial gallons per mile	Litres per kilometre	2.82481
Litres per kilometre	US gallons per mile	0.425144
US gallons per mile	Litres per kilometre	2.35215
Volume		
Imperial gallons	Litres	4.54596
Litres	Imperial gallons	0.219975
US gallons	Litres	3.78531
Litres	US gallons	0.264179
Imperial gallons	US gallons	1.20095
US gallons	Imperial gallons	0.832674
Cubic centimetres	Cubic inches	0.06102
Cubic inches	Cubic centimetres	16.3871
Imperial gallons	Cubic feet	0.160544
Cubic feet	Imperial gallons	6.22883
US gallons	Cubic feet	0.133681
Cubic feet	US Gallons	7.48052
Litres	Imperial pints	1.75980
Imperial pints	Litres	0.568246
Litres	US pints	2.11344
US pints	Litres	0.473163
Distance		
Feet	Metres	0.3048
Metres	Feet	3.28084
Miles	Nautical miles	0.868976
Nautical miles	Miles	1.15078
Miles	Kilometres	1.609344
Kilometres	Miles	0.621371
Weight		
Pounds (lbs) 1-99	Kilograms	0.454
Pounds (lbs) 100-999	Kilograms	0.4536
Pounds (lbs) 1000-9999	Kilograms	0.45359
Pounds (lbs) 10,000+	Kilograms	0.453592
Kilograms 1-99	Pounds (lbs)	2.205
Kilograms 100-999	Pounds (lbs)	2.2046
Kilograms 1000-9999	Pounds (lbs)	2.20462

To convert: Centigrade to Fahrenheit: (°C x 9/5) + 32
Fahrenheit to Centigrade: (°F - 32) x 5/9
For normal climate temperatures for °F, double °C and add 30.

Finally:

50 mph = 80 km/hr